ALCOHOL RECOVERY

A Complete Recovery Guide for the Addicted to Alcohol

(Learn How to Regain Self-awareness to Change Your Alcoholic Habits)

Wesley Woodard

Published By Chris David

Wesley Woodard

All Rights Reserved

Alcohol Recovery: A Complete Recovery Guide for the Addicted to Alcohol (Learn How to Regain Self-awareness to Change Your Alcoholic Habits)

ISBN 978-1-77485-296-5

All rights reserved. No part of this guide may be reproduced in any form without permission in writing from the publisher except in the case of brief quotations embodied in critical articles or reviews.

Legal & Disclaimer

The information contained in this book is not designed to replace or take the place of any form of medicine or professional medical advice. The information in this book has been provided for educational and entertainment purposes only.

The information contained in this book has been compiled from sources deemed reliable, and it is accurate to the best of the Author's knowledge; however, the Author cannot guarantee its accuracy and validity and cannot be held liable for any errors or omissions. Changes are periodically made to this book. You must consult your doctor or get professional medical advice before using any of the suggested remedies, techniques, or information in this book.

Upon using the information contained in this book, you agree to hold harmless the Author from and against any damages, costs, and expenses, including any legal fees potentially resulting from the application of any of the information provided by this guide. This disclaimer applies to any damages or injury caused by the use and application, whether directly or indirectly, of any advice or information presented, whether for breach of contract, tort, negligence, personal injury, criminal intent, or under any other cause of action.

You agree to accept all risks of using the information presented inside this book. You need to consult a professional medical practitioner in order to ensure you are both able and healthy enough to participate in this program.

TABLE OF CONTENTS

INTRODUCTION 1

CHAPTER 1: WHAT TO KNOW IF YOU'RE AFRAID OF ALCOHOL 4

CHAPTER 2: ALCOHOLISM & RECOVERY STEPS 12

CHAPTER 3: WHAT ARE THE BAD THINGS ABOUT ALCOHOL 34

CHAPTER 4: THE PATH TO TREATMENT AND RECOVERY .. 42

CHAPTER 5: FINDING THE WAY OUT 52

CHAPTER 6: MANAGE YOUR CRAVINGS, AND TRIGGERS . 74

CHAPTER 7: SETTING GOALS, AND MAKING CHANGES 78

CHAPTER 8: HIRE A THERAPIST 84

CHAPTER 9: WHAT IS IT SO HARD TO STOP ALCOHOL? 97

CHAPTER 10: FORGET ASSISTANCE 105

CHAPTER 11: JUST ONE GLASS AT ONE TIME: HOW TO REDUCE THE AMOUNT OF ALCOHOL YOU CONSUME 112

CHAPTER 12: THE NEGATIVES OF ALCOHOL/WHY YOU SHOULD NOT DRINK 124

CHAPTER 13: RESTITUTION 142

CHAPTER 14: UNDERSTANDING ALCOHOL 152

CHAPTER 15: DEALING WITH PEER PRESSURE 167

CHAPTER 16: ALCOHOL WITHDRAWAL SYNDROME 175

CONCLUSION **183**

Introduction

This book is ideal for everyone:

If you're looking to cut down or stop drinking alcohol for health and fitness reasons,

If you are looking to cut down on the amount of alcohol you consume,

If you have to quit drinking alcohol due to different reasons,

If you're looking to end your acohol dependence, then you should consider acohol

...and lots more.

There are many ways to identify alcohol addiction The severity of the disorder demonstrates the frequency with which people drink alcohol and the kinds of alcohol consumed can vary between individuals; Some individuals are heavy drinkers others drink, and remain sober for a while.

Alcohol addiction, also referred to as alcoholism is a disease which affects people from all different walks of life. Experts have tried to pinpoint the influence of genetics, sex competition, socio-economics, and so on that can trigger individuals to become addicted to alcohol. However, there is no sole cause, however it is possible that psychological, genetic, and even behavioral issues can play a role in the development of addiction.

It is important to recognize the fact that addiction to alcohol is a serious diseasethat could impact your brain and mind So, a person suffering from an addiction to alcohol may not be able to regulate their actions.

Once the body has been freed from the negative effects of alcohol consumption The body will then begin to recover.

This is particularly true for drinking because they are by definition subconscious thoughts processes. With his meticulous study of the most current neuroscience research and his own journey through the world of addiction, this Author is able to crack the code of changing habits by addressing the ways in which habits develop. This innovative and unique technique has allowed thousands of people to change their drinking habits easily and without pain.

Chapter 1: What To Know If You're Afraid Of Alcohol

Although numerous studies confirm the negative impacts of drinking too much alcohol however, the number of people affected by this problem is on the rise. As per the Centers for Disease and Prevention over half of the US population of 18 and above is a regular alcohol drinker. In 2013 there were 18,136 instances of deaths due to alcoholic liver disease and 29,001 alcohol-related deaths, which excludes accidents and murders. When alcohol-related incidents are considered the picture gets worse.

It's admittedly, a little difficult to measure the amount of alcohol needed to be consumed to determine whether it is an indicator of alcohol dependence. It is true that people do differ in their tolerance to alcohol levels.

However, addiction, whether for alcohol or any other substance isn't only measured by the quantity or intensity of the substance. More important is the way in which the consumption or use of an addictive behavior or substance can trigger many debilitating effects for the person who is addicted.

How do you tell when your consumption of alcohol has been past the limit of acceptable levels? The following signs indicate of an alcohol dependence

1. A lot of times, the urge to drink is uncontrollable.

In normal situations, you should not be compelled to drink alcohol.

However, the scenario is different if you have an addiction to alcohol. It is possible that you are not able to resist the urge to take a drink. When you feel the need to drink, that desire is so intense that it is almost impossible to resist. Therefore you can stop everything you're doing and forget about the negative effects of drinking.

2. The denial of the reality

Most often, alcoholics not admit to having an addiction at all or even quit drinking when they feel the need to. The fact that you deny there's an issue is capable of continuing to do whatever you're doing (in this instance drinking) without being ashamed, guilty or embarrassed. It's a defense system that allows you to keep feeding your addiction.

3. A higher tolerance to alcohol

If you're dependent on alcohol You may notice that you need to drink more and more alcohol to experience its effects. This is because , as you continue drinking the alcohol, your tolerance grows. The body becomes accustomed to alcohol after a time and, as a result, you don't notice any significant consequences unless you continue to increase your consumption.

4. Double life

Despite their repeated self-denials people who drink realize that they have an issue. This is why they might keep this part of their lives a secret to those closest to them. They don't want relatives, friends or coworkers to be aware that they drink heavily because they fear being judged, dismissed from their job or even asked to stop the habit. In the end, they have two lives: one where they seem to be normal, and another where they drink without restriction.

5. The cycle of guilt and self-hate

Sometimes, you might acknowledge that you are suffering from a problem and continue drinking, but with a guilt-conscious. Perhaps you also had hoped to maintain your sobriety for a long time and began the path to recovery, but then fall apart and fall off later after you gave into the urge to drink. After the enjoyment of drinking has diminished it is then that guilt and shame come back. The cycle could go for a long time, and result in a sour view of the self-worth of your own, depleted confidence and a low self-esteem. If you're addicted to drugs to alcohol, you might experience the cycle of self-hate and guilt.

6. Lower productivity

When they spend a lot of time in a bar or getting an overdose The amount and quality of alcohol-related alcoholics productivity at work or at home could be negatively affected. This could hinder the development of their professional career and cause negative consequences for the relationship of the sufferer with those around them. You may have seen it in your personal experience.

7. Legal issues can be a source of tension.

In certain instances, prolonged consumption of alcohol can cause more impulsive and compulsive behaviors which could lead to impaired decision-making. If left unchecked these characteristics can result in violations of the law.

8. Alcohol as a method to let yourself relax

It is possible that you've fallen into the habit of regularly drinking alcohol for relaxation, perhaps after a tiring day at work or after a dispute with a close friend. If drinking alcohol has become your "go-to" way to relax and feeling more relaxed, it could be a clear indication of alcoholism.

9. Do you drink more than you had planned?

Before you begin drinking, you could be thinking to yourself "I'm just going to have one drink, perhaps two". If you regularly exceed the limits of your body, this could be a sign of alcoholism.

10. Feeling withdrawal symptoms

The next chapter will discuss the signs of withdrawal that alcoholics experience when they quit drinking. If you're an alcohol user, you might begin to feel certain symptoms even in the absence of drinking. They could include fatigue, headache, difficulty sleeping and irritability as well as depression shaking, anxiety, and shakiness. It is also possible to use alcohol to deal with the symptoms you're experiencing.

11. Blackouts

If you drink frequently to the point that you suffer blackouts (can't recall what transpired for a duration of time your drinking) it is possible that you have an addiction to alcohol.

12. Family and friends are concerned about you.

Our friends and family are the ones that know us the best, and often more than we do. If your family members or your acquaintances express concerns about your drinking habits it could be a signal to be concerned and determine if you are suffering from an addiction.

The things listed above are the most frequent signs of addiction to alcohol. Other indicators could be financial issues caused by excessive drinking as well as a shabby appearance, inability of focusing and a depressed emotional state.

There are many alcohol-related self-tests which can assist in determining the extent to which you are suffering from an addiction to alcohol. They are all available online and could be beneficial but it is advised that you speak with your physician to conduct an appropriate evaluation.

What is it that causes addiction? This question will be addressed within the following chapter.

Chapter 2: Alcoholism & Recovery Steps

4 phases of addiction development

In the year 1960, biostatistician and researcher on the effects of alcohol Elvin Morton Jellinek (E. M. Jellinek) was a hit after he published The condition notion for alcoholism. It offered new perspectives to look at addiction to alcohol.

Jellinek saw addiction as an ongoing relapsing disease which must be treated by medical researchers and developed a theory about how addiction develops over different stages. The model, which is now widely accepted, outlined the theoretical stages of addiction to alcohol that each was viewed as having a distinct change in physical, mental and interpersonal relationships.

Do not assume that all people suffering from drinking alcohol go through these phases These steps can be helpful to assess the amount of alcohol consumed and avoid potential issues. The four stages of alcohol dependence are:

Pre-Alcoholic: The first step is drinking alcohol for the first time, which is when tolerance to alcohol increases when a person starts to drink more frequently, which is an approach to deal with stress, anxiety or other emotional issues.

The Early Phase: Jellinek sees this as the stage of transition where the formation of a cyclical pattern of abuse begins. Drinking more frequently becomes more common, and people start using social events as a reason to drink. It is also possible that they will drink alcohol in order to treat negative effects of drinking, like hangovers. In the present blackouts can also happen.

Middle Stage The Middle Stage is the most crucial stage of Jellinek's theory which is why when a person begins drinking regularly and frequently or even begin their day with one or two glasses. They may have difficulty maintaining relationships with family and friends, or even become irrational in their behavior. It is possible that they will experience health issues like hangovers, nausea or a shaky stomach.

The past due stage This final phase causes a complete losing control of drinking. The person is required to consume alcohol. At this point the body begins to seek out alcohol in order for normal functioning. If the person doesn't drink regularly it is possible that they will experience withdrawal symptoms as well as extreme cravings.

Risk Factors for Alcohol Dependence

Many factors, including genes, family history, the environment, and mental health factors can affect whether an individual develops an alcohol dependence disorder. The way these factors affect the risk of a person isn't fully known. Certain people have multiple risk factors, but do not increase AUD, whereas others may not be unique risk factors but do have an issue with alcohol use.

Certain factors that are believed to be contributing to the possibility of developing an alcohol-related addiction or dependency on alcohol are:

Environment: Children being raised by parents who regularly consume alcohol are more likely to be more likely to be influenced by this behavior in a different way than children who were raised in homes that are alcohol-free. Other influences in the environment, such as the pressure of peers, siblings and other family members could contribute. People who have been victimized or neglected, or went through domestic violence are at more danger of developing alcohol-related issues later in life.

Genetics: The effect of genes isn't fully understood However, experts have pointed out that the reasons for this include a high tolerance to alcohol, a desire for alcohol, and a tendency to be dependent on alcohol can be passed on from parents to their children. Researchers have estimated that genes are responsible for around 40-60% of an individual's likelihood of having a craving for alcohol, as well as external factors.

Genetic and ethnicity-related physiological variations In addition to genetics, there are other factors that influence a person's likelihood of developing an obsession. Four studies of the effects of alcohol consumption on people from diverse ethnic groups have revealed that some are more likely to drink less due to specific enzymatic differences in the body's capacity to eliminate and detoxify alcohol. For instance numerous Asians suffer from skin flushes, nausea, headaches and other unpleasant effects after drinking, regardless of gender. Women are more likely to be more vulnerable to negative effects of alcohol more than males.

Mental Health: Those with mental health issues (e.g. depressive disorder panic, depressive disorder) who use alcohol to ease their pain are at a higher likelihood of becoming a victim of AUD than people with no pre-existing health issues. Around 43.4million adult adults aged 18 and over had some type of mental illness in the year 2015.

What do you know if Alcoholism diagnosed?

The Countrywide Institute on Alcoholics beverages Abuse and Alcoholism (NIAAA) identified the disorder of alcohol consumption as compulsive drinkers where the drinker is unable to control their consumption or to stay clear of alcohol and is experiencing negative emotions even when they are not drinking.

The Diagnostic and Statistical Manual of Mental Disorders (DSM-5) provides 11 criteria for the diagnosis and treatment of people suffering from alcohol dependence. If someone is exhibiting any two symptoms in the space of 12 months they may be suffering from an AUD.

What is an effective treatment?

In the mid-1970s, research revealed a variety of concepts that are vital in creating the fundamentals of any successful treatment. Treatment could involve medication to ease withdrawal symptoms; therapy via an intervention program for rehabilitation to help understand the problem and alter behaviors as well as a long-term program of aftercare such as group therapy to aid in maintaining sobriety and preventing the relapse.

It is important to recognize that the same approach won't be effective for all people, so treatment plans should be reviewed and altered depending on the patient's evolving requirements. Effective treatment can focus on more than just addiction to alcohol and could be able to address the needs of mental disorders that could be a cause. Studies show that treatment for at least 90 days can bring positive results.

What is the point at which it becomes alcohol dependence?

The experience of watching a family member or a friend who suffers from an AUD may be a challenge. It is possible to ask, how could you do to set things better or resolve the issue? And how do you convince the person that they need assistance.

Alcoholism is the word used to define someone who suffers from an AUD. A person who is addicted has both a mental and physical dependence on alcohol. They may have issues controlling their drinking habits, or continue to drink even when it is causing issues. These issues could impact their professional and social relationships and their health.

A disorder of alcohol can range from mild to extreme. Moderate patterns can turn into grave problems. The early treatment can help those with alcohol dependence to reduce its extent. Although it is up to the individual to decide to stop drinking but you can assist and encourage them to do so. Learn about the actions you can take to assist your family member, friend or loved one.

How to beat alcohol-related Disorder

The first step is to learn about alcohol abuse and alcohol consumption.

Before you take any action it is important to know whether your loved one is dependent on alcohol. Alcoholism, also known as AUD is simply drinking excessive amounts of alcohol at every opportunity. In some cases, drinking alcohol to alleviate anxiety or to enjoy social events could turn into alcoholism, however it is important to recognize that there are two distinct concepts. People with AUD shouldn't drink in small amounts. To know more about the condition, read about the symptoms of alcoholism and how it manifests.

There are government-run programs and websites that provide more details on how to help someone suffering from addiction to alcohol. Look these up for more details on cravings and the experience it brings:

Al-Anon.

Alcoholics Anonymous.

SAMHSA

The Countrywide Institute for Alcohol abuse and Alcoholism

Second step 2: Do what you're saying

Let the person you care for be aware of your love and how you love them. Make sure to use words that are positive and encouraging. Avoid being hurtful, harmful or arrogant.

The use of "I" minimizes complaints and lets you be seen as an important participant in the conversation. It is beneficial to talk about a particular issue or issue, for instance, the time when drinking alcohol caused an unwelcome effect like physical violence or financial difficulties. Instead of telling someone, "You're an alcoholic - you must seek help right now," you can say, "I love you, and I value you If you want to know. I'm concerned about the amount you've consumed, and it's affecting the health of your family."

Be prepared for any response. No matter what the response is, try to remain calm as you assure loved ones of your love and respect.

Step 3: Select the most convenient time and location

Pick the ideal moment and time when the mood is there to have this important conversation. Pick the location that is secure and private. It is also important to stay clear of interruptions, which implies that you'll need the attention of each other. Be sure that you're not angry or distracted by other things.

Step 4: Strategize and concentrate on compassion and honesty

If you're struggling with alcohol, the most important aspect to consider is be honest and open about the issue.

Tell your loved one that you're worried they've been drinking a bit too much, and inform them that you're willing to help your loved one in getting rid of the habit. Be prepared for a negative reaction. Make sure to not show any opposition to your findings An average person would be unable to deny it and may even respond with anger. Be patient with their responses allow them the some time and space to consider itand then listen to what they've got to say.

Step 5: Provide your assistance

You shouldn't try to force anyone who doesn't require treatment to receive one. The best thing you can do is provide assistance and be helpful. It's up to them decide if they'll take it. Be compassionate, unprejudiced and authentic. Imagine your self in the exact position and think about what your reaction could be.

The actions you take are more important than the words. Always show them that you value you and encourage them to seek treatment at the hospital. Be consistent and stick with them.

You might want to find out whether your family or friends should be involved. It could depend on a variety of factors, like how serious the situation is as well as how closed the individual is.

Step 6:

Talking to you about issues is different from getting involved. The treatment process is inclusive and includes planning, providing results by sharing information, and selecting the best treatment option.

Intervention is important when the patient is unable to get assistance or treatment. It is a way for family, friends as well as coworkers can confront the person and urge the person to seek treatment. Interventions are usually done in conjunction with counsellors. A trained therapist is able to:

Help on ways to help the person enter treatment.

Discuss the treatment options available.

The Signs of Alcoholism

Alcohol-related behaviors can be difficult to identify, but unlike heroin or cocaine; however, alcohol is readily available and it is a common practice in various societies. It's usually the foundation of social relationships and is usually associated to celebrations and enjoyment.

Alcohol consumption is a fundamental element of the lives of some and for others they are influenced by the culture, but it's hard to tell the difference between someone who drinks often and those who are addicted to it.

The signs of addiction to alcohol include:

Increase the quantity of food consumed.

Alcohol tolerance is high.

Drinking alcohol in inappropriate times and locations.

Are you looking to be at a place an area where lots of alcohol is e.g at a gathering, party, etc.

Change in friendship: Someone who is a drinker may pick people who consume a lot of alcohol.

Beware of interactions between family members.

Refusing to admit or deny the fact that you have drank alcohol.

Depend on alcohol for perform work or to engage in the activities.

Professional or legal issues such as arrests or loss of a job.

The effects of addiction get worse over time it is important to recognize early enough symptoms of addiction (if diagnosed and treated quickly) If you are who is addicted to alcohol would likely ignore the symptoms.

If you're concerned that somebody you're familiar with is dependent on alcohol, you should avoid making them feel shamed by making them feel ashamed. This may cause them to withdraw from you or cause them to be resistant to your help, instead be encouraging and reassuring them.

Medical Conditions that are Associated with alcoholism

The addiction to alcohol can cause liver and coronary heart diseases, and it could result in:

Ulcer.

Diabetes.

Sexual issues.

Congenital disabilities.

Bone loss.

Eye problems.

Cancer risk is higher.

Immune suppression.

Alcohol addiction sufferers is able to risk others' lives due to their insidious state. Based on the statistics of the Centres for Disease Control and Avoidance (CDC) approximately 28,000 individuals in the U.S have been killed as a result of suicide or homicide. This is largely due to alcoholism.

This is a good reason why it is important to address alcohol dependence early. Nearly all issues related to cravings for alcohol could be avoided or addressed with long-term rehabilitation.

Treatment Strategies for alcoholism?

The treatment for addiction to alcohol can be a difficult and complicated. In order for treatment to be effective and be effective, those suffering from addiction must abstain from drinking the alcohol they can or cut down on their intake. You shouldn't try to force the person to stop drinking when they're not prepared. Treatment success is dependent on the patient's desire to get better.

The recovery process for alcoholism is long-term and arduous and there is no quick fix that is not a continuous maintenance; as a result of this, many believe that people suffering from alcoholism do not ever "healed."

Rehabilitation

A common option for those suffering from addiction to alcohol is either inpatient or outpatient program. A program for inpatients could last for anywhere from 30 days to a year; it typically reduces the symptoms of drawback and psychological issues. Outpatient care provides support throughout the day and allows patients to return home.

Alcoholics Anonymous and other Organizations

Alcohol-dependent individuals and are in need of help may want to consider a 12-step program similar to Alcoholics Anonymous (AA); certain organizations do not follow the 12-step system but instead choose to go with Wise Recovery or Sober Recovery.

Whatever your support system is the support system is, it's important to try to remain sober. The sobriety can help those struggling with an addiction to alcohol. An environment that is welcoming could provide relatable stories and solid and healthy assistance; these can aid an alcohol addict and give them a comfort when they experience the possibility of return.

Other Options

Alcohol addicts might also benefit of various treatments like:

Drug therapy.

Counseling.

Food-related changes.

Doctors can prescribe medications to treat specific conditions, e.g, antidepressants. Antidepressants are effective if the person who is addicted to alcohol is taking self-medication for his or her depression or when doctors prescribe medications to help with other ailments that are associated with recovery.

It is simple to go to sessions with a therapist to educate one in determining the best way to manage any strain that may occur in recovery, and how to stay away from repeat relapse. In addition, healthy eating could aid in repairing any harm that drinking alcohol has done to one's health such as regaining weight.

The treatment for alcohol dependence can involve a variety of treatment strategies. A person suffering from addiction should enroll in one of these programs that can help support the long-term recovery process; it could be a session of therapy for someone who is typically depressed.

Where can I find assistance in the fight against alcoholism?

To learn more about alcoholism or to assist those you love to help them It is recommended to speak with a doctor. They could refer you to local programs, like programs like the 12 step program or centers. Additionally, the below organizations might be helpful:

National Council on Alcoholism and Medication Dependence (NCADD).

National Institute on Alcohol consumption Abuse and Alcoholism (NIAAA).

National Institute on Drug abuse.

The drug abuse industry and the Mental Health Services Administration.

What's the view on alcoholism?

Treatment for alcohol dependence early is advised since addictions that last longer are harder to conquer However, the most effective treatment is designed to help long-term habitual behavior.

Family members and relatives of those who are alcoholics can offer them professional assistance or sign up for programs such as Al-Anon.

An individual suffering from addiction to alcohol who has been sober for a period of time or even years could be able to recognize that they're experiencing an episode of relapse. This may be the result of the habit of drinking to excess. At some point, sobriety might be the responsibility of any person who is addicted to alcohol.

It's crucial to avoid encouraging harmful behaviours and to keep reasonable limits if an addicted person continues to drink. this could mean cutting off the financial aid if it would cause them to be unable to satisfy their desire.

If you know someone who is addicted, try to motivate them and provide emotional assistance.

Chapter 3: What Are The Bad Things About Alcohol

Drink with caution - do you consider the warning as a serious matter? Get closer to the significance behind those words of caution. Find out what happens to your health when you believe that you are immune to the negative effects of alcohol.

Heart Disease

It is possible that you have heard about alcohol lowering the chance of developing heart disease. However, this isn't the whole truth.

Researchers have discovered that drinking a glass or two every day boosts HDL cholesterol, which is a substance found in blood that can help to reduce the amount of fat in your body. Take a deep breath! Before you make that an excuse to drink your drink, remember that it is only effective if it is consumed

OCCASSIONALLY. If you go over the daily limit, alcohol can be harmful.

Don't believe what you read regarding the alcohol's HDL production capacity. Instead, think about this that drinking too much increases the likelihood of getting cardiovascular and blood disorders. Alcohol sucks up fats from your bloodstream, damages blood vessels, increases the blood pressure and could even damage your heart. Alcohol can be fatal to you. Remember that.

Stroke

The blood is affected by alcohol by decreasing its capacity for creating blood clots. Additionally, it increases the risk to cause blood vessels within the brain to break and leak blood.

In the event of this the stroke is hemorrhagic and it is much more deadly than an ischemic stroke which is caused by blood clot within the brain.

In spite of the fact that your blood is less clot-proof and less likely to suffer from an stroke that is ischemic, you're still at risk of having a hemorrhagic stroke. Write this down in your mind that alcohol = stroke = Disability or death. Remember, strokes don't always kill.

Cancer

Mouth and throat cancers are frequent among those who drink, especially those who drink more than four glasses of alcohol per day. More importantly drinking at least two drinks per day are more prone to developing colon cancer. Women's breasts are not immune from the cancerous effects of alcohol. female drinkers are 40 percent more likely be diagnosed with breast cancer. Cancer is likely to surface everywhere within your body, especially when you frequently drown your cells in poison.

Diabetes

There's a new and confusing fact regarding alcohol: it can help to reduce the risk of diabetes, however, it can also cause it to worsen.

Alcohol drinkers WHO drink moderately are about 30 percent less likely than those who do not to develop diabetes as a result of the following potential causes: alcohol appears to trigger cells to respond more efficiently to insulin and also slows food absorption , making the levels of insulin more manageable.

However, if you go over a certain threshold and you're not able to benefit from its properties to fight diabetes. You'll gain weight due to the alcohol's calories, consume more food, and consequently become heavier, more obese and develop obesity-related ailments such as diabetes, if you don't already have it.

What's wrong going on with diabetes, you may ask?

When you get it, you'll suffer from damaged organs in your body, particularly the kidneys and your heart. It is also possible to go blind or have your limbs removed when the wounds you've suffered don't heal. If you're already suffering from diabetes, you must avoid it. Drinking too much alcohol can cause you to feel hypoglycemic, such as the feeling of being sick and seizures, as well as unconsciousness or brain damage, and, of course, death.

Dehydration

Alcohol and water aren't compatible You can test this the difference yourself by mixing colored liquor with clear water. You'll notice that they split into layers after a time. This is also true for your body. The more alcohol you consume and drink, your body will absorb more fluids to spit out. This is why you'll pee more often after drinking.

If you do this for long enough you'll be losing a significant amount of water and it will cause you to dehydrate. Do you think dehydration isn't something to worry about? Here's the consequences of losing body fluids:

* Uncomfort

* Unrest

* Inability to cry (this could be uncomfortable and painful)

* Splitting headaches

* Feeling helpless

There is a general feeling of weakness throughout your body

* Persistent nausea

* Confused

* Fainting spells

* Unconsciousness

* Possible death

* Malnutrition

Alcoholic drinks contain calories in the drinks. Drinking a lot of them makes your body believe that you're full, and therefore are no longer hungry. The problem is that the calories you ate do not have the essential nutrients that your body needs , so you're left with a lack of nutrition.

Additionally, alcohol can be injurious to the interior that line your digestive system. It makes your digestion function poorly. There are times when you have to throw your food and it is an expense that was spent on food, and valuable nutrients.

Birth defects and miscarriages

Alcohol is distributed throughout your body through your bloodstream. It also travels into the uterus. If you're expecting, you can be sure that your child's unborn baby will taste your drink too.

He'll also expose him to risks of alcohol, including malnutrition, dehydration, blood poisoning and many more.

Drinking while pregnant? You can expect to have an infant who is underweight and possibly birth problems. Also, it's possible to have your baby born too early or suffer an unplanned miscarriage.

If you've been successful in staying away from alcohol even while carrying a baby within your womb. Don't end the battle now. Alcohol can also make its way into breastmilk, so it's advisable to stay clear from alcohol. It's actually better to stay clear of drinking in the case of parents of a child who is young. This way you'll be better able to take care of the child.

Chapter 4: The Path To Treatment And Recovery

The path to recovery and complete recovery from alcohol can be a difficult one. Like we said, the majority of people who are weaning off alcohol go through a period called the withdrawal phase. This is particularly true of those who have developed physical dependence to alcohol. The most frequently reported symptoms experienced during the withdrawal include shaking, sweating, headaches nausea or vomiting, anxiety, insomnia as well as insomnia, diarrhea, difficulties concentrating, higher blood pressure and an elevated heart rate and pulse.

The withdrawal phase begins from just a few hours during which you're unable to drink. The symptoms may get worse within 2 or 3 days. Some alcoholics suffer from severe withdrawal symptoms. These symptoms may be so severe they can be life-threatening. Some of the most dangerous withdrawal symptoms are:

Disorientation and confusion severe

Chills and high fever

The vomiting is severe and frequent.

Extremely agitated and hallucinations

Convulsions and seizures

If you are experiencing some of the above symptoms contact for assistance immediately. If you're unable to manage your symptoms, dial 911 or any other emergency number in your area or country to seek help.

How do you deal with the withdrawal signs at home

If you are able to control the withdrawal symptoms, and believe you are able to manage treatment at home , then you may want to begin your the process of removing alcohol at your home.

The process of creating a withdrawal strategy

You require a powerful plan to guide you through your day-to-day activities when you are slowly abstaining from drinking alcohol. The plan will outline your actions throughout the week and the strategies for staying sober and manage your cravings. Here are some suggestions for creating your own plan.

Find out what is triggering your drinking addiction and take steps to stop it. If you drink to are looking to relax, you may want to take part in other activities to alleviate stress. If you drink to go to this establishment each day after work, it's an appropriate time to find a different way to go. The bottom line is that anything that can trigger your drinking needs to be eliminated.

Make a short-term plan as well as a long-term one too. The short plan must be a daily routine and can be as simple as avoiding drinking alcohol throughout the day. Every day that you're capable of achieving your goal , note this in the blog or in a journal. The act of writing it down will motivate you to be a better person every single day. However your long-term plans include overcoming the addiction to alcohol for a period of a year or more. Plan your long-term goals imaginative to help you be more inspired:

Find a way to make amends with your spouse or your partner

Take a look at your child's ballet recital and be in a safe, sober environment.

Replay basketball

Get back to work.

What can you do to reach your objectives? You can't do nothing and wait for it to happen. It requires lots of effort and therefore, you must write specific steps you need to take to meet each goal in the short term and, eventually, to meet your objective. For instance, your main aim is to go to your daughter's wedding in a clean state. Each day you will maintain your sobriety for a day at an time. You want to stay clear of alcohol on a daily basis. To achieve these short and long-term goals, these tips can be helpful:

Do not trigger yourself; this will happen day after day.

Speak to a friend or family member about your plans and strategy.

Share your plans via social media and set an annual countdown to get to your main objective.

Get involved in activities, fitness and eat well.

Make time to pray and communicate with God.

Make your drinking plans each day at a time. Some suggest that it's ideal to stop abruptly, however some experts suggest that a gradual method to stop drinking will help you to do it more easily and to prevent withdrawal symptoms. It is up to you to determine which approach is most suitable for you.

Do you prefer cold turkey or gradually weaning?

Which approach to avoid alcohol do you believe is the most effective for you? Each strategy has its own benefits and drawbacks. Find out which is the best fit for you using this comparison:

Pros and cons of cold turkey

Makes you quit right away. You won't be touching any, sensing, or tasting alcohol for the remainder of your withdrawal process and your treatment.

Focus on your goals immediately and you can start your treatment, recovery, and withdrawal when you are prepared.

You could be at risk being afflicted by withdrawal symptoms, so you need to be motivated to implement this method.

There is a great chance of getting drunk again, however If you're extremely motivated and have a solid support system, it is possible to stay clean for the length of time you will.

The gradual withdrawal method has pros and cons

You'll taper how much alcohol you consume slowly until you're no more drinking. The most popular method is to cut your consumption in half , and then stay at least 4 or 5 days before cutting the amount by half for another 4 or 5 days , and the cycle continues.

There is a lower chance of experiencing withdrawal symptoms when you follow an gradual withdrawal from alcohol.

It's not simple to apply this method as you must have total control. It is generally performed with the guidance of a counselor or the buddy system.

You must know the amount of alcohol contained in your drink since it's distinct from one drink to the next.

Whatever method of treatment you select it is important to be aware that recovery is only two steps away. The process of withdrawal should not be undertaken by yourself; instead, you should reach out to your family members and friends to seek help.

It is also important to take breaks from work, school or work to allow yourself to fully get over the effects of alcohol. If you can, inform your workplace or school that you will have to stop working for a minimum of two weeks. So, you'll be less distracted and will have more control over your reactions in response to treatments and withdrawal.

Relieving withdrawal symptoms

If possible get medical attention If you think you're having trouble getting rid of alcohol. It is also important to talk with those you trust regularly. Here are some suggestions to help manage some typical withdrawal symptoms:

Avoid operating machinery or driving and the more you focus, the more likely you are to experience fine tremors and shaking. Relax and take a break. Participate in activities that aid in relaxation like swimming, sports biking, jogging, or dancing.

If you experience nausea, avoid eating the entire meal. Instead, eat small meals frequently. Drink light snacks and eat crackers. freshly squeezed fruit juices. Avoid drinking caffeinated drinks as they can only make you feel more agitated.

Take more fluids. Hydration can reduce dehydration that occurs as the result of nausea or diarrhoea.

You can reduce stress through stress relieving activities like meditation, yoga breathing exercises, yoga, and many other. Reduce stress prior to going to bed so that you can rest comfortably. Keep a record of your stress levels and recovery from alcohol. Write down everything you experience and how you managed to cope with your issues. You'll find it is much easier to fall asleep when you put aside your anxieties and worries prior to.

Find support networks to manage other withdrawal symptoms, such as anxiety, insomnia and stress. Focus groups allow you to stay in touch with others who have similar issues as you do and offer support too.

Chapter 5: Finding The Way Out

Then, we came to the core issue: "What to do?"

While it is true that this question is correct the question has no meaning. It is obvious what to do: don't drink! A lot of people fall victim to this specific trick. Incessantly answering questions like: "What to do?" and "Who is responsible?" These people wander in the dark, walking around in circles, searching for something beneath their feet but are unable to locate it because they don't know what it's like.

The question needs to be asked with a new perspective: "How?" How do you avoid drinking to those who are who is afflicted by the illness which is the cause of his actions?

Many people will answer immediately: "How! Drink no alcohol and that's all!" Let's nevertheless move away from superficial opinions and stop looking at the issue in a primitive way and start to comprehend: "It's simple, but it's not an easy task." You shouldn't suggest someone who is a drinker to show his strength: "You are a man!" "You are a strong woman!" In no case do you offer values as reasons such as: "You have a family!", "You have an office in the public sector!" Do not set the conditions: "Throw away the drinks and buy a summer home."

The decision must be taken exactly like that! We've said before that there is no logic.

If this choice is made then the most crucial aspect starts. A person with this kind of status has lots of difficult and challenging, yet interesting work. The task is to comprehend the place you are in and where you're not yet. You must know yourself, so that you can determine the manifestations that you had and which ones have come from the this disease.

It is crucial to recognize that discussing the possibility of a cure is not acceptable.

Dependence, once it has infiltrated the soul, will never leave it. However, this doesn't mean there aren't individuals who have quit drinking. There are a lot of them who drink a great deal however, they aren't previously alcoholics, but those who have learned to not follow the rules of alcoholism.

It is a matter of a technique that has been meticulously taught, and not just in a single session, so it is not a guarantee. it. It is a skill only those who are able to learn by themselves acquires. It is not true, and there are no tablets that have the skill , or even acquiring the ability "by by proxy." Then, there is the ability that anybody can learn. There isn't someone who is studying, but not learning.

If there is nothing to show for it this means that he hasn't begun any project so far. Also, as I said earlier that it's simple however, it isn't easy.

The most important suggestion should be "Start discussing this issue!"

A lot of people, upon hearing this, are puzzled. Evidently, our brains are so created that "thought originates from our mouths." A person will never be able to understand what's happening until he makes it clear as the word. When he calls it demons, people manage to remove their influence. I am focusing on influences, and not the thoughts themselves. These thoughts are likely to occur many times in this soul.

Most often, you will are told: "Make sure that there isn't any traction!"

To be exact The patient is able to feel that "craving" of compulsive desire right before the break. This condition encompasses all desires. As generally, it becomes impossible to stay clear of the consumption. Also, Traction is a condition in which there is no other option.

If someone is experiencing cravings, that means it's not too for them to be late. When the craving does not appear it is not felt. It is discovered that to the question

"How do you feel?" The patients answer: "No craving!" Absolutely not! If there were a desire then we would have been aware. You can take steps to ensure that there isn't any pull. This is the outcome which must be achieved.

There has ever been a pill, injection, or other method to manage desires. It's frightening to think what could happen if someone could alter the desires of another at their own discretion. The demand "remove the desire" involves merely removing one desire, but leaving the other ones.

In the majority of cases, when you hear about "flushing" in the liver and purifying our body "toxins" and then repressing "stress," a person might lose their traction. In general the "miracles" are provided by experts from the fields of resuscitation, toxicology or even by people who do not have anything to have anything to do with medical treatment. If you consider this suggestion, it might be the case that if an person who is responsible for the offense rinses his liver, then will he be a saint? Unlikely.

Most of the time, all these tricks are employed by a sick conscience to bargain.

Of course your internal organs in an alcohol-dependent were severely affected. And, of course, drops and preparations for the liver are suggested for those suffering from liver disease. However, to think that this can eliminate cravings is not a good idea.

Certain drugs trigger alcohol intolerance. The therapy is known as sensitization. There are opinions on these techniques that are mixed. Some doctors or patients who've quit drinking alcohol think that these techniques are unacceptably, because the chance of dying in the case of a breakdown during treatment is too high and unworth the outcome that patients receive. However, some, in the opposite insist that other patients are not able to cope and provide regular medical attention.

In the beginning, I'd like to know more about these techniques. The therapy isn't new , and like every other business is now rumored to be discussed.

In the beginning the first point, these substances don't eliminate the urge to drink, but makes it difficult. They are not centrally acting or psychotropic, tranquilizing or antipsychotic.

The second issue is that the sarcasm of those who say: "how so, I consumed alcohol and didn't pass away!" is not quite obvious. What is better in the event that he did die? He was, after all, an experienced doctor with a great reputation and thought you would take a drink?

The inhumanity is when people convince "friends" who have received medical treatment that they claim "you can drink, and you aren't going to be dead!" I immediately want to know: "and if he dies will you take responsibility in the demise of your close friend?" Yes, there isn't a

100% guarantee in medicine. However, a person may have three or two reactions to alcohol, and a person could be disabled by the first drink.

In any event, everyone should be aware of the fact that these manipulations are just an insurance policy to help you get started. You cannot file the capability to swim. There aren't any injections that require the ability to speak the language of another. If I completed the process - great job and well done. This is a method that merits admiration. However, this is only the beginning. Think about the possibility of giving crutches. But not for a long time, but for one year. If you begin walking using crutches, maybe you'll give up at the time. However, if you've been doing anything to keep sober and you'll eventually lose the habit.

The most common scenario is "hard-drinking within one year." It is an individual who received medical treatment just a year ago. The term is now expired and he's walked to the bar. When asked "what was your life like when you weren't drinking?" The answer: "I was working extremely hard all week long for twelve months of the year." When you ask "What were you doing to stay sober?" You will receive the following answer: "I was not drawn. I did not experience any cravings whatsoever. Let's go back to medical treatment for a year. Then, after one year, we'll have another meeting."

It is crucial to realize that this isn't the result. Sometimes even wives get offended. What a beautiful life! Every year, you have to bear the life of a person "on the platoon" fearful that one day there will be a binge. keep track of the days, and when that occurs, feel terror and dismay!

The virtue of sobriety is an important quality, if it is by a trusted person. It's like getting married. If you only marry once per year, no one can claim that you're a man of the family.

A lot of people often ask: "And for how long should you quit?" This is not an easy one. Some believe that it's better to begin by using short phrases: half a year or a year. If everything went well, you can extend it to three or five years. A lot of experts believe that If you were able to convince that patient to undergo the treatment for the full duration, you should begin at five years. To support this there is a clause that within a year you won't have the time to comprehend anything.

The conclusion is that if someone has followed it for 3 years and then after a year, the procedure was broken the procedure, it does not have any logic for more than an entire year.

The best option is that the individual determine the time that is evident to him, and the time frame he can think of. It is important to note for a person who needs binders for the next 25 years they typically inquire: "Can you imagine what you'll be when you reach the age of 25?" Usually, people respond: "What are you, to me, three years is infinite!"

Essentially, getting out of the fog is not a matter of jumping. Simply place your feet in clear location. It's more pleasing to know that the person who has received the medical precautions for six months, and at the conclusion of the period comes in to consult about whether he is able to perform the procedure for the next year. It is crucial that following the time of drug's action there was no break. As you ascend to the top of the staircase, the primary aspect is to not slide down, but to walk slowly, but do not to walk back up.

Even after I've completed the process it is essential to start the most crucial aspect - to master the skills that were previously described.

The process should begin at the beginning of your first day of recovery, and should not be stopped.

Schools of Sobriety - A step towards becoming a person who is able to Drink.

Maintaining sobriety is an essential ability, then surely there are schools that can help you learn it? Yes, there are "schools." This book will talk about a handful of them and not because all aren't good, but because the story could be infinite.

We've discussed before that the most important thing to consider is to be able to speak about this topic in a non-intoxicated manner. Conversations should take place in a private environment since their primary goal is to ensure absolute, unwavering transparency in one's self. Anyone with whom I am able to be honest with should inspire faith in me. There is no reverence or submission, but faith. I have to be certain they won't apply what I have did against them.

The conversations discussed should be seen as a form of manipulation for medical purposes, or the advice of a physician. It is not advisable to delay them because of external reasons. It's similar to a wound dressing. If the doctor told us to do it twice every two days We would wrap the wound once twice a day. Uncertain of the reason, but not being able to think, why do we need to bandage so often. This suggestion should be followed regardless of whether the patient is on an excursion for business or is exhausted.

I'm not going to speak about this issue or, more precisely I don't wish to talk about it! It won't be working immediately; conversations will appear absurd and meaningless. It may at first appear as if there is nothing to gain from these conversations. We have agreed - this is a talent. It is important to keep practicing. Not necessarily immediately, but to be successful in all circumstances.

The most effective method of conducting these conversations with your family. Many patients were fortunate; they have been able in saving their family members. Family members are the ones who you can trust. is no reason to hide things from them, and especially illness.

It is recommended to do this at least every week. In reality, the more frequently you do it, the more effective. The reality is that development of dependence can take anywhere from one to two weeks and so, when we attempt to comprehend our own behavior in the span of a month, it is possible to avoid it.

The procedure should be incorporated into the family routine: each week, on a pre-determined day (usually prior to the weekend, though there aren't any specific guidelines) within our family we need to discuss how we are doing on this particular front. In general the conversations are held by spouses, however I was interested to know the way in which the patient spoke to children of adulthood or a person with whom they were on fishing trips or even in bathhouses.

Rule one

In the course of conversation there is only one subject being talked about - the disease. The following sentences are not acceptable: "I don't want to talk about this issue!" "Enough to shame me!" "There are more important issues!" There is no more vital topic for a patient. If you're suffering from illness, there's no reason to be ashamed. We are here to show compassion, so let's take action! The most common scenario is that: they started with the most important thing, and eventually, they lost track of things happening around the world or a vacation home with family members. Thus, we quickly set the next hour, say between 21:00 and 22:00 - solely about the illness, about you and your family members.

Rule two

In the course of discussion, you must talk about feelings, not just events. It is often the case that we believe that the events of life are linked to feelings. For instance, when responding to the question "How did your day go?" You hear: "I was up at

5am at work, then was at work for a while, went back to my home, ate dinner, watched television, and finally went to sleep." It's a professional police report. It is now clear what time and where I was, however what I was feeling isn't completely clear. The day's description could be like the following: "I woke up in positive spirits, with spring was in the air, birds were outside my window, I was ready to get to work. I went for a walk with joy. After arriving at the station, I realized that it was Thursday and I was thinking Friday would be an unofficial day! It was a shock to me and didn't want to do anything. I was working "on my machine." After lunch, I felt nausea. I'm already going home, but I was thinking that something else should be completed. Today, I'm contemplating whether I should make a phone call to someone I don't have a connection with." It is important to note that there weren't any unusual circumstances, but what a variety of feelings! This is the topic we're supposed to discuss.

I'd want to point out the reality that some people try to use words to describe their feelings like frustration, sadness and so on. It is more beneficial to speak those terms that you know. It is not necessary to appear shy. If someone declares: "Covered, flattened, drag," ..." it's far more powerful than the cutesy "depression" without knowing what it actually means.

Rule three

It is important to speak to someone. It's unlikely that someone will be in a position to speak up to the other person. To know the truth of what you say to yourself, it is necessary to gaze at those eyes you're speaking to.

The outcome of this discussion should result in an understanding of what your health is currently. If "everything is well," there is no problem, then something's been concealed, and you have you have lied to yourself, and tried to make yourself appear more attractive, and not cause any disturbance. This means that the illness is in the back. It does not show up, but it's alive. This is a highly risky scenario, as you aren't able to see the problem, so it's easy for it to get it.

What is the most frequent time you need to see a patient who's wife was gone yesterday, hasn't been working for a week, likely dismissed, there's an unclean apartment and when asked his question "How is your life going?" He responds: "Everything is fine! Don't worry!" Now, if I had heard: "Doctor, I have problems!" I would become less anxious.

Unfortunately, these conversations within the family aren't always a reality. This is not because the family is poor, but because the emotions and thoughts that are associated with the illness look like they are so terrible that they are sad for their loved relatives. It's frightening to think that they'll be worried about the things they hear. One patient has shared the following story: "My wife went to meet with my relatives, but she's late and I'm concerned. This isn't unusual. Then, at once I was thinking what if she'd had an accident? Then, could you imagine, a flood of joy washed over me. I'm at home alone I am grieving I'm able to drink! There is no one to blame!" He said that even an unwelcome cold sweat had poured out. "What an insane person is I, when the traumatic experience or even the death of my wife's beloved brings me back to having a drink!" It's clear what you should not immediately decide about telling your dear ones. However, you'll still have to let them know. If not, the worms could change into snakes.

In these cases There are spaces that patients can gather to discuss their issues with each other. These are referred to as rehabilitation programs. My opinion is that the concept isn't particularly efficient. First of all, the term "rehabilitation" in a lot of countries has been associated with the political meaning for quite some time and secondly, the term "program" has a resemblance to working on a computer more than a person's soul. However, that's just my opinion. And the word itself has been ingrained and is not worth changing.

The most important requirement for these programs is privacy. There is no secret or mystery. that is, anonymity as an element of security, because no one know who the other one is. So, in these groups, you can speak up about what is bothering them, without fear of being judged.

The most well-known and widely accepted program is the program "12 steps" or" Alcoholics Anonymous. The major benefit of this group is the fact that it was developed not by academics but people who are alcoholics. It is not the result of research conducted by scientists however, it is the result of knowledge gained from experience. It is the experience of those who took action to help. The program is a long-standing one in the true sense, and has been thoroughly tested and been proven to be a method that more than one person achieved the desired result. In the present, "12 steps" is an international phenomenon that doesn't have any clear indications of a nation-wide mindset. The program is extremely versatile and well-tested. We'll go into more detail in the near future however for now, you should be aware that there's an area, but it's not the only one.

Furthermore there are many other programs. In several cities, you will find numerous places to receive this assistance.

Furthermore there are those who have been sworn with an oathand which states that they will not reveal their identity to anyone. Talking with them can also be held in a secure environment. Sometimes , you will hear misunderstandings of the concept of medical confidentiality. The doctors said that they would never reveal any information to patients. Additionally, throughout the globe, there's this kind of specialty, namely psychologists. They are not any medical training, however they also claim to be anonymous in their help and pledge to keep the secret.

In the end, there are those that are held to a very old swearing. This is the case with clergymen of the church. In all religions of the past confession is a matter of faith. is acknowledged. Alcoholism is believed to instil the spirit the spirit of an evil spirit. It is believed that a person who is drunk is obsessed with demons and a person who is sober and has had such experiences is haunted by demons. The demon is clever is a sleight of hand and is not a compulsion but is always enticed to hide and deceives. The most important thing is that the demon is scared of truth and he's indestructible. The only option: each day throughout life to be awed by the purity of your thoughts and intentions, and then compare them with the desires of the Most High.

I'd like to bring attention to the truth that there aren't conflicts between medicine and old-fashioned beliefs of the human race regarding God. Actually, we're talking about the same thing, however, the words are different.

Chapter 6: Manage Your Cravings, And Triggers

There is a chance that you will have intense cravings for alcohol, particularly in the first few months following you've made the decision to quit drinking. The recovery plan you have created should include strategies for how to manage the cravings that come up. It is important to consider several strategies that will assist you in coping with pressure from social and stress and relapse back into drinking and your desire for alcohol.

One of the most beneficial options is to be aware of the triggers for your desire. It could mean that you need to change certain things in your social circle. It could be necessary to say goodbye to your drinking buddies to ensure that you won't be enticed to drink once more. It is also important to know how to tell "no" in the event that it is attending a gathering where alcohol is served.

Here are some strategies you can use to curb your alcohol cravings:

Send the thoughts, feelings and ideas with someone you are confident in.

Take your focus off other activities while allowing your cravings go. You could go out for a walk. It is possible to finish your washing or talk to your friend.

Be sure to inform yourself of the numerous advantages and reasons you shouldn't drink.

Recognize your cravings ("urge browsing") and let it to flow. Do not resist or ignore the urges.

How to Perform Urge-Surfing

Be aware of and consider your craving. This can be done by selecting a comfortable chair in which you can put your feet in a flat position on the floor. Put both hands into a comfortable position. Inhale deeply and exhale for a few times , and keep your attention on the inside. Your focus should be directed through all the various parts in your body. Find out which area of your body is experiencing the desire for alcohol and how the cravings feel like. For example, you might notice that you feel the desire in your mouth and are eager to take the drink. Perhaps you feel your heart beating faster due to the desire.

Pay attention to one area of your body that you feel the craving. If you decide to focus on your mouth, be aware of the different sensations you feel within that body part. Does your mouth feel dry? Do you feel it is hot? Are the muscles surrounding and inside it relaxed or tight? Do you think about the way alcohol tastes on your mouth and in your throat? Do you take more in?

Concentrate on the body parts that are experiencing cravings for alcohol. Keep in mind that the goal of this exercise is not to fight your cravings instead, but to allow it to go on. Just observe how cravings change. If you continue to practice craving surfing, you'll eventually master it effortlessly and your cravings will less easily go away from your body.

Chapter 7: Setting Goals, And Making Changes

You've now made the decision to make a commitment! I am sure that you have observed that there isn't benefits to drinking. That is the reason you're here; thank you! After you've taken this decision it is time to focus into a goals-setting process. This is in relation to drinking and how you intend to stop drinking and quit. It is essential to set objectives and actions to follow that is clear and achievableand the best approach to manage.

You might want to cut down and completely stop drinking at once, however it isn't always possible when you've been drinking for a long period of time. If you are in this situation, you will need to make gradually reduced drinking levels until you are able to stop all at once. Consider quitting drinking on certain days during the week. You could decide that there is no drinking during the first phase on Sundays. Then, you can move up by adding Saturdays as a no-drinking day. You'll notice that you'll progress as this and after three months you will not have any desire to drink. In any case, if you drink regularly, you can decide to stopping drinking in two-day phases.

After you've made this decision, then you must determine what day you'd prefer to reduce your drinking or quit and stop. This could be the next day, or a week later one month, even after a half year. Indicating the date of your quit is a crucial idea. If you can do this in writing, it makes the process more efficient. This can add value and allow you to actually achieve the goals and plans.

Other things to think about are ways to resist the temptation that may arise along the way, methods you can announce your goals to your family members and also acquaintances, methods of getting the public to know the new limits on alcohol consumption and how to avoid the negative influences that be a part of the process, and drawing inspiration from your previous experiences while drinking.

There will be temptations in the course of time However, removing all items that are related to alcohol from your home and office is highly recommended, this will include bottles of alcohol and barware for your home. Make sure that your family, colleagues and acquaintances know that you've made the decision to stop drinking. If there are any who might be drinking, tell them to stay away from your home to prevent them from tempting you.

It is possible to decide to go to any event with alcohol as well as to be with the "former" drinking companions. Distinguishing yourself from individuals who do not offer the support you need to make your choice can be very beneficial. This puts more effort to your plans. If that means you have to give up your social life and friendships, then allow it! The lessons you have learned from previous attempts to cut down on drinking can be a good way to start. You'll be aware of what failed and what has worked. Also, it will provide several good strategies for "pitfalls" to avoid.

Do we need to stop drinking completely or gradually reduce drinking?

Examining the extent of issues that arise from drinking is the most appropriate answer to this question. This could include assessing the amount of hours you've been drinking, the type of alcohol you consume your time, how long you've been drinking and what you do with your friends, just to name some instances. It is also crucial to be aware that alcoholism implies that you're unable to maintain a healthy control of your drinking habits and drinking itself. Therefore, for any alcohol-dependent person, it is important to take a stand and stop drinking in a group.

As per the National Institute of Alcohol abuse and Alcoholism The National Institute on Alcohol Abuse and Alcoholism, making a choice to stop drinking is recommended in cases where you are looking to stop drinking because of health and personal reasons. This gives both your body and your brain time to adapt to the new circumstances and eliminate the anxiety related to drinking. Consider setting up a self-drink strategy or goal can be effective. In the past, you made your choice to drink two bottles daily and then get to one bottle, then half at the end, you will be able to quickly stop. Writing down your plan makes it effective.

Another way of dealing with the situation is to keep a drink diary. Note in your diary every moment you had a drink, including days, weeks, and months in addition to the quantity of drinks you consumed and your friends who were involved participating in the drinking. Make sure that the diary records an improvement in your drinking. Be sure to not keep any alcohol in your home, or just keep a small amount which is small.

It is recommended that you eat snacks prior to drinking. If you are drinking alcohol in conjunction with soda, juice or water can cause it possible to drink only an insignificant quantity of alcohol. The other thing to take into consideration is taking breaks during every drink and stopping at a certain moment and recharging. In the time between breaks, which could be for a couple of days, allow yourself time to rate your feelings as well as the way the physical feeling is. It will be extremely easy to quit drinking once you've succeeded and you feel good!

Chapter 8: Hire A Therapist

Therapy is different from other types of treatment since when you are in therapy, you are under the guidance of a trained professional. There are many kinds of therapy available to help with the effects of alcohol. I'll only cover the cognitive-based type of therapy since it's without doubt the best.

The concept of Cognitive Behavioral Therapy(CBT) is founded on the belief that emotions and behavior are triggered by beliefs and the way in which one perceives the world. Self-destructive behaviors aren't founded on factual information but is a result of an individual's past experiences as well as his beliefs he has learned and the fully developed coping strategies.

The therapy is focused on thinking and the belief that, even if not able to change your situation it is possible to change the way you view them , and how you behave.

CBT helps you understand the link between emotions, thoughts, and actions, and the impact this connection has on recovery. It is commonly used to treat addiction, as well as in other disorders, such as eating disorders and attention deficit disorder anxiety, bipolar disorder and PTSD. CBT has been proven to be effective when utilized on its own. But, according to the National Institute of Drug Abuse, CBT had been shown to be extremely effective when paired with support groups and medications.

How does it work

If you decide to sign up for CBT when you sign up for CBT, you are made to believe that a lot of your choices are not right and a majority of your beliefs and emotions result not from actual facts but rather from your past experiences and the environment.

It's vital to know why you are feeling the way you do and behave in a particular manner, and the way that these influences affect your addiction. You'll be better prepared to overcome your impulsive behavior and to plan your way out. Your therapist will work with you to alter your behavior response to negative thoughts, and thus end the cycle of drinking binge.

The first step is to recognize the negative thoughts you have. The negative thoughts you have are known as "Automatic Negative thoughts" and they're usually a result of misinformation because of your childhood and self-doubt and anxiety. The thoughts that accompany them and their horrible feelings are often responsible for the development of depression and anxiety that is a hallmark of clinical depression. It could be the root of your alcohol-related problems as you drink to eliminate the thoughts that are negative and unpleasant emotions.

CBT concentrates on the thoughts and emotions that drive your addiction as well as your reactions and instinctive behavior. It teaches you to look at your thoughts more closely instead of simply acknowledging them, changing the way you speak to yourself, and finally choosing different actions every time you encounter an automatic idea.

For the treatment of addiction to alcohol, the objectives of CBT both you and the therapist collaborate on include:

Rejecting false beliefs that lead to excessive drinking

Training in skills to boost your mood

Scheduling when to participate in non-drug related activities

The ability to identify and avoid situations that could cause alcohol dependence

Understanding the internal and external triggers that trigger the desire for alcohol and binge drinking

Knowing what relapses are and how to deal with it.

CBT comprises two major parts;

1. Functional analysis

The therapist you see works with you to pinpoint the feelings, thoughts and situations that led to and after drinking. Over time, you could realize that your emotions and thoughts are due to an abuse incident in your childhood and a long-held myth or false memories , and alcohol is merely a way to cope.

You could also discover that it's because of an old practice of beating oneself up whenever you commit a mistake, or believe that you cannot be alone, which causes you to continually seek the services of others. These ideas and more could result in alcohol-related disorders.

Functional analysis will allow you to determine what you think about, and why you take drugs initially. The ways you go about it and the circumstances that could cause the relapse.

2. Training for skills

The next step is to develop more effective thinking skills and how to respond better in response to thoughts. Therapists help you to break the old habits and assist you develop healthy habits and skills. You are taught to speak more positively to yourself, praising yourself for little achievements and also to inspire yourself more by thinking about the effect of alcohol consumption to your entire family. You discover new strategies to deal with the situations and thoughts which led to drinking in the past.

Additionally, you are taught specific techniques for behavior like - not talking back to thoughts that trigger negative emotions and not planning parties or going to a bar in the event that you are tempted to drink alcohol, deciding on another route for your evening walk if it leads you towards the bars, picking an example in your area and following their steps.

As you will observe, CBT goes beyond just giving your heart to a patient therapist. It's more of a goal-oriented therapy that is focused on the short-term issues. Your Therapist and you work in tandem on specific skill development to help you overcome your addiction. While other types of therapy aren't as stimulating and take a long time. The process will end after taking 12-16 scheduled sessions that last between 60 and 90 days in rehab programs that are planned.

CBT can also be adapted, so you can do your sessions from your home or even in an inpatient facility. CBT can be practiced at home, at the office , or in an environment with a group of people.

The 12 step method

Cognitive-behavioral methods are specifically designed exercises designed to help you think more clearly as well as managing triggers properly and acquiring better behavior. It's common to be taught a variety of essential techniques over the course of 12 sessions.

Sessions 1 through 3

In the initial three sessions, you'll learn to acknowledge that you have a problem while acknowledging the difficulty and seeking assistance. The program will guide you in identification of the common mental thinking patterns and the root causes of your troubles. The habits that cause addiction and addiction, and you'll begin making the necessary changes to counter these patterns and thoughts.

Session 4

Session four is about creating an inventory of the negative feelings, triggers and impulse-driven behaviors, everything that you can change and then setting goals to help you recover and live an improved life.

Session 5-7

The sessions are designed to help you develop an open dialogue with loved ones and open communication to get over the addiction. You discuss your issues with your therapist. You are encouraged to form friendships with your supportive friends and your family.

Session 8-10

These sessions help you develop skills focused on improving your current situation through addressing previous mistakes and making necessary changes. These sessions concentrate on the reflection of mistakes that were made during addiction as well as the negative experiences those you loved. The goal is to recognize these errors, and make the necessary corrections, and make amends to any mistakes that may have occurred.

Session 11-12

In the final session you will learn how to cope better and develop empowering practices, while also sharing your experiences with others. The sharing of your experiences either in private or group sessions helps you overcome the struggles and strengthens your recovery.

During the time you go through these sessions you will learn various social and psychological techniques to aid in your recovery. The main techniques are

1. Examining the mind

In depression and an anxiety state, the thoughts seem to make no sense. There are generally patterns to these thoughts. You feel that you're not good enough and that you are the cause of negative things happening to you, and you believe that bad things will occur.

It's absurd because no one is born with a bad character or fated to have a bad destiny. But the experiences of life can cause you to form a variety of beliefs that alter your perception. CBT is a method of observing your thoughts and combating your thoughts with alcohol rather than drinking them up.

The purpose is to record arguments against and in support of your ideas and assist you to make sense of your thoughts.

If you're fond of drinking alcohol after work the underlying reason could be "I'm an idiot lacking any expertise and my boss is right to say I don't have capabilities, and I ought to take more alcohol to combat my pathetic existence".

After reviewing the facts, that idea changes to " I do have abilities even if my boss doesn't know it yet. I will always be able to learn by listening to his advice, and take lessons from my mistakes. I don't require alcohol."

The more you consider the facts, while keeping a cool mind, the more likely you are to quit beating yourself up and will be able to make better ways to respond to your thoughts automatic that will result in better choices.

2. Exposure to light based on the visual

In this workout it is suggested that you frequently recall painful experiences. Refraining from memories that are painful is a vicious cycle , and the more you keep them away by drinking, the more they are able to dominate you.

Your CBT therapist will urge you to consider those memories that cause negative emotions. It is a requirement to expose yourself to the details of the sounds, sight and the emotions that are triggered by the moment. This could happen when you were subject to abuse in your childhood or when you're bullied or make an awful error.

When you expose yourself to the negative image and letting it go, it loses power over you, and anxiety decreases with time. It's an easy procedure that takes the courage to do it. Your therapist will provide that courage. It works because fear is an illusion. The more you take action to overcome what you are afraid of the more you can overcame the fear.

3. Behavioral experiments

The process of behavioural therapy involves altering how you respond to negative feelings and thoughts to discover which triggers the change. Some people gain more from self-kindness, forgiveness and love. Some people benefit from letting themselves experience some hard loving and self-criticism. This is different for each person. Your therapist will work together with you to select the method that is most effective for you.

4. A pleasant schedule of activities

The process involved making an agenda of enjoyable and healthy activities that keep you busy and also to ward off impulsive behaviors. Instead of drinking while working, you should be advised to sleep in and listen to relaxing music. You can play games on the internet with your children instead of having a party with your friends.

These tasks should be straightforward and simple to complete. When you plan them out you can limit your risk of triggers and the subsequent desire to drink.

Chapter 9: What Is It So Hard To Stop Alcohol?

When confronted with a drinking issue the first thing the majority of people will desire to do is find effective methods to stop drinking. But the fact about the situation is these suggestions do not discuss the reasons why it is difficult to stop drinking in the beginning. Perhaps the most effective method for getting rid of alcohol is to identify what is the root of the issue. You'll find many sources arguing that you should begin with setting goals for yourself as well as drinking in a controlled manner, watching for pressure from peers or seeking help. It's possible that this isn't enough to address the root of the issue. Therefore, this section will outline some of the reasons it's typically a major task to give up.

Letting Go of Your Favorite Friendship

There are a variety of frequent experiences that anyone who's suffered from alcoholism will the witness of. From the moment you consumed alcohol you realized that you had made an acquaintance. For shy people drinking alcohol may give them the confidence they'll be able to adapt with new social groups. If you are drinking more and the more you drink, the more alcohol can expose you to new people. In some ways, it works as a confident friend that is always at hand to ensure you're enjoying yourself. It can help you get over your shyness in dating. After a time you'll gain the fame you've always wanted. You won't be as isolated like you were in the past.

From afar, drinking alcohol is an effective problem solver. Your self-esteem, which you struggled with will increase in the same way. You are well-known among your peers. That's what people desire. The knowledge that alcohol will provide you this chance but at the expense of being drunk is why the majority of people glued to their drinks.

Unfortunately, the bond you build with alcohol doesn't last for long. Sure, you may have relied on alcohol in different situations however, in the end you'll realize that you cannot live without it. It is possible to go out with your buddies even when you're not sober and it is a nightmare. Sure, you'll be bored to the point of exhaustion and the next thing you'll notice is that you'll have to ask for a glass just to let you out of your secluded mind.

Why is it so hard to quit? One of the major reasons you'll be unable to stop is that you'll be leaving of your most trusted friend. It was a friend who was always there to help you through many difficult situations, a problem-solver or an arm to rest on, and you can be certain that they will snuggle you into bed to sleep.

The fear of giving up is what makes the majority of people be hesitant to quit drinking. We face the uncertainty of what happens after the time comes to stop drinking. We aren't certain if we'll be able to keep the friendships we once enjoyed. Everything that goes into remaining sober is undiscovered. It is possible that this makes people reluctant to make changes to improve their lives.

Recognizing the Problem

Another reason that addicts are unable to get off is due to their inability to acknowledge they have an issue. This is referred to as being in denial. The victim is usually insecure about their drinking habits. It shouldn't be a surprise to them to say that they are able to end the habit should they wish to. This is a typical excuse they offer to their friends and family.

Other people will be aware of the problem However, they are hesitant to give up. In this scenario it is possible that someone tried to stop drinking before, but was unsuccessful. The consequences that they felt are what made them reluctant to move in this direction.

Changes in Brain Chemistry

People who have tried to stop drinking but fail will blame themselves. They find themselves thinking they're failing because they can't quit without seeking help. One thing you must know is that cutting out alcohol goes beyond the desire to do it. It's much more than just your desire to quit drinking. In simple terms your brain is altered. The positive side is that you can take back control and transform your life.

The addiction to alcohol has many complex elements that affect the brain in complex ways. The experience that addicts endure and their path to addiction differ. But the aftermath effects are similar. A few drinks can give one an uplifting and peaceful mood. Individuals who engage in frequent drinking can have temporary changes to their brains.

However, drinking regular alcohol and in large amounts alters the brain's chemistry in profound ways. This creates a difficult job to control your drinking habits. In time, you'll get into a cycle of it feels like you require more alcohol to achieve similar effects. This causes your to boost the amount of alcohol you drink and the frequency with which you drink. In turn, the result is that alcohol can alter the way your brain works. This will also affect the way you feel.

In the present, prolonged consumption of alcohol is likely to alter your brain's chemical. Then, your brain may no longer function the way it did in the past. The result is an environment where you have to consume alcohol to be normal. Consider it this way that the urge for alcohol consumption is as when you're hungry. The more you attempt to put off eating and eat, the more you're in the grip of hunger. It's hard to ignore these aches.

Don't be a victim of yourself because you've failed your efforts to get rid of drinking. The most important thing to remember is that your brain is significantly affected. Your request for help will make an impact on your recovery.

The fear of recovery

There's always a negative view about rehabilitation. This creates fear in people who are addicted. In turn, this serves as a further reason why addicts are hesitant to take the necessary steps to get better. The idea that there are unpleasant withdrawal symptoms that you could endure can deter those who are the idea of quitting alcohol.

The truth is it's difficult to stop drinking alcohol if you're already addicted. But, it is important to be aware that it is doable. There is a variety of treatment facilities where you can seek medical aid. These professionals are experts and are aware of the best ways to aid you in detoxing. The good thing is the fact that you can avail medicines available to help you with withdrawal symptoms.

When you look at the bright side, it is important to realize that there's nothing negative that could happen. Sure, you'll encounter a variety of unpleasant events however, you'll be able to go back to living your life. You will be freeing you from the shackles that drinking has created to hold your mind captive.

There is no doubt that alcohol addiction can lead to an addiction that is difficult to quit. The hardest decision you can ever make , considering that you'll be saying goodbye to a person whom you've been with for years. Additionally, considering that you'll have to fight to control your thoughts, this means that you have to be committed to the process. If you're looking to become sober, the best time to take a step is now. Don't put your body at risk any longer. Get up and get the assistance you require.

Chapter 10: Forget Assistance

Support from family as well as friends, doctors and therapists can be helpful throughout your journey. You rarely encounter someone who is doing this on their own. Supporting a group will aid you in making the decision, then go through the process, and then continue it throughout the remainder of your existence. Sometimes, joining support groups for alcohol dependence is an additional step you should do to reach that ultimate objective of complete sobriety. Being able to connect with others who have experienced what you're going through can ease your burdens of fear, anxiety and depression. anxiety.

Alcoholics Anonymous

The AA group is among the most popular and widely accessible groups around the globe. The objective of AA is complete abstinence from alcohol and they follow a

12-step plan to assist you in not just reach this goal but also keep it throughout your entire life. It is the Twelve Steps of Alcoholic Anonymous:

We acknowledged that we had no control over alcohol and that our lives had become too difficult to manage.

I was convinced that a higher power than us could restore our sanity.

The decision was made to hand our lives and our will over to the trust of God in the way we saw the God we worshipped.

We took a thorough and unflinching moral assessment of ourselves.

Recognizing to God and to ourselves as well as to another fellow human, the particulars of our mistakes.

We are completely ready to see God take away all of these flaws of character.

I begged Him to take away our imperfections.

Created a list of everyone we'd been hurt, and then decided to apologize to everyone.

Redressed directly with these individuals as often as possible, except in cases where it would cause harm to them or other people.

We continued to conduct personal inventories and when we made a mistake, we quickly admitted to it.

Prayer and meditation to enhance our awareness with God and to better understand Him by praying only to be aware of His plans for us, and the power to fulfill that will.

After experiencing an awakening in our spirituality due to these steps, we set out to pass on this message out to alcohol users and also to apply the principles of these Steps in all of our activities.

If you're looking for a local group check out their website at www.aa.org

SMART Recovery

SMART Recovery is a fantastic support group offering four-point program for overcoming alcohol dependence and other forms of addiction. SMART Recovery sponsors face-to-face meetings across the globe and regular online sessions, meaning you will always have someone to help you in times of need it. They also have chat rooms online as well as an online chat room that is available 24/7.

The four-point program:

Inspiring and Keeping Motivation

How to deal with Urges

Controlling thoughts, feelings and Behaviours

Maintaining a Balanced Lifestyle

To find out more visit www.smartrecovery.org

Women For Sobriety, Inc

Women For Society, Inc. is a non-profit organisation that is dedicated to helping women recover from alcoholism and other addictions. Established in 1976, the WFS Program grew out of one woman's desire to be sober. The program focuses on 13 affirmations "New Life" Acceptance Program:

I'm suffering from a life-threatening condition that I had previously.

Negative thoughts only harm me.

The habit of happiness is something that I will build.

My problems are only a problem in the sense that I allow them to.

I am who I think.

It's possible to be boring, or great.

Love is a powerful force that can alter the direction of my life.

The main goal of our lives is spiritual and emotional growth.

The past is over forever.

Every love that is given will return.

Exuberance is my main exercise.

I am a capable woman with a lot to contribute to the world.

I am accountable to myself as well as for the actions I take.

For more information visit www.womenforsobriety.org

Secular Organizations for Sobriety

SOS is an internationally-based non-profit organization that focuses on recovery using the use of science and self-empowering. They provide a different option for those who may be not comfortable with the religious and spiritual aspects of other recovery programs that are available. They prefer to praise the person for achieving an undying commitment to sobriety, without the assistance of an outside source.

They host gatherings in cities around the globe. If you are looking to locate the nearest one, go to www.sossobriety.org

There are many recovery organizations around the globe So, do plenty of research to find the one that meets your requirements. Contact other members, and maybe visit several before you decide which one you prefer to join. Keep in mind that this must be a place that you feel at ease and to trust their principles so that you are able to completely absorb yourself into their mission.

You also have the possibility of choosing a group that provides online courses if you're in a position to not meet in person. Many prefer to begin online classes before meeting face-to-face. Or even doing both. They both offer benefits, and both will give you an excellent service.

Chapter 11: Just One Glass At One Time: How To Reduce The Amount Of Alcohol You Consume

So, you've decided to instead of going cold turkey' and avoiding all alcohol You've decided to cut down on your alcohol consumption? Awesome. It could lead to the elimination of alcohol altogether Maybe it won't. It isn't a matter of concern. Every person has their own personal desires that they'd like attain and, rather than saying the goals you have set are nonsense and not achievable, you have connect with others who are there to assist you on your way.

I've separated this section into two sections cutting down your drinking alcohol at home and, reducing drinking alcohol while going out for a night.

The heart is where home is. Then there's the booze.

Imagine the scene you've just come home from a long 11-hour workday. You're exhausted, your work was a disaster and you're ready to unwind. You curl up on the couch in front of the television and put a microwave-ready food in, and then pour yourself an ice cold glass of wine. It's a huge glass of wine: after all, this was a very stress-filled day.

There is nothing wrong with it in any way. In fact, I've done it several times. Sometimes we require to sip a glass of wine front of the television. Have you thought about how a bottle of wine at the evening of a Monday' could quickly become a two glasses of wine Monday, Wednesday , and Friday', and then suddenly it's two bottles of wine every week'. It's possible to sneak into your life and, before you realize it, you've earned yourself an alcohol dependence. Here are some suggestions and tricks that are conscious and some subliminal that can assist you in reducing your alcohol consumption. that you drink every week.

Buy smaller wine glasses. Have you ever sip an enormous glass of wine then glanced at the bottle and thought , 'Wow! That's nearly the whole bottle gone and you're not even sure what it was? If you have only tiny wine glasses in your cupboard, all you'll pour yourself is a tiny glass - there's no need to fill it up, simply because there's no room!

Purchase an alcohol measuring device. If you're at home pouring your spirits You just make your best guess as to the amount of spirit you'll pour into your glass, don't? Studies have proven that people who drink at home are more likely to over-pour their drinks by as much as 50 percent. The 'single' that you have poured yourself could be closer to an entire double. A measure of alcohol will allow you to keep the exact amount of spirit you add to your drink, and will help you cut down on your consumption.

Drinking alcohol after dinner. What is the best time to drink? If you're lying on your sofa, watching the latest episode of your favorite TV show? Do you consider your evening to be your "drinking time"? Meaning that nothing else can get accomplished because you'll be distracted (or intoxicated) in order to complete anything else than drinking? So, why limit your drinking to just dinner? There is a time limit to relax and drink and the food will soak up alcohol, which means you won't feel its effects more; plus you'll be able to limit the amount of alcohol and wine you consume while enjoying your meal.

Replace Replace Replace! It may sound easy, but the most effective method to reduce your consumption of alcohol can be done by...not taking a sip of alcohol! If you're not tempted to reach for a drink instead, why not try an iced drink? Perhaps tea? Find the non-alcoholic beverage you love: there are many available!

Change your drinking habits. What is the most likely time to be drinking at home? If you're bored? If you're watching TV? Make it a different channel! Find something else that won't provide you with time or the time to have a drink. Walk or take a bath or engage in a pastime. These may at first appear like distraction methods however, after a few weeks and with continued practice you'll realize that the routine that encouraged drinking is gone. In the blink of an eye, you'll start witnessing significant improvements in all aspects of your well-being!

Make a budget for your alcohol. With alcohol readily available and affordable in some instances it's quite simple to buy one additional bottle' for the right amount. Make a budget for each month's consumption in order to (this is the most difficult part) adhere to it! You'll not only reduce your consumption of alcohol and consuming, but you'll also save cash too!

Time for a Party Time

Have you been invited to join your buddies to an evening of heavy drinking? Instead of completely refusing, you've opted to go along however, you're concerned about how much you'll end with? Sure, you'd like to have a great time however, can you have a fun night out and not drink the same amount? Of course you can! Here are some ideas and strategies on how you can still have fun however, you should limit your consumption of alcohol.

Keep your eyes on the ball. Here's a classic scenario and I'd like you to admit it when you've done it. You've just begun drinking on your night out , and you don't feel like you're drunk yet and you choose to drink more quickly to feel the buzz more quickly. After 30 minutes the feeling hits you at once. Then, all of a sudden you're drunk. Are you familiar with this scenario? This is the point where the concept of keeping yourself on your toes is a good idea. The human body requires about 1 hour to digest 1 unit of alcohol. That means that it takes around 2 hours to complete the process of the equivalent of a pint. If you consume a large amount of alcohol at once it will put too much stress on your liver and could be at risk of serious health issues. By keeping yourself on a schedule and spreading out those alcohol units over a longer time and giving your body time to process it properly. If you're out drinking, stop between drinks and make the most of them! Then, go to your next steps...

Alternate! I'm the kind of person who likes to drink a glass of wine on hand whenever I'm out. It can be tea, water vodka, vodka, or whatever so long that I have some alcohol to consume. It is usually something alcohol-based, however, we face the same problems as being a good pacing while drinking. Instead, you should alternate between two soft drinks as well as an alcohol drink when drinking. A tip to remember: every when you're ordering drinks at the bar, request for an ice-cold glass in addition. After you've finished your usual drink and are done, there's the water glass waiting for you. The act of drinking multiple drinks can prolong the duration of your night drinking (as you don't go overboard early) and minimizes the chance of having an excessive hangover early in the morning.

Get used to soft drinks. Do you remember a drunk friend who you tried to get sober by presenting drinking a glass of water in the disguise of alcohol in order to convince them to drink? Doesn't work, does it? It tastes just like water. If they're saying , 'I want some lemonade and vodka from the bar' think about getting them regular lemonade instead. It's a good idea! It's true! And it could work for you as well! If you're not an avid big fan of water or soda, then (whilst you're mixing your drinks, obviously) opt for an alcoholic drink instead. It's a good idea because in the event that you don't want others to be aware that you're drinking less it looks as a vodka-lemonade. person will be able to tell the difference!

Eat! It's obvious, however eating food while drinking will help reduce your effects from a hangover. Also, it will fill you up that you'll drink less. This is because food is able to absorb a significant amount of the alcohol that is in your body, which means that you don't have as many toxic toxins moving around your stomach. If you're planning on going out drinking in the evening, make sure you eat a big dinner before drinking - - something heavy and loaded with carbohydrates. If you're going to go on long-distance drinking be sure to go to an eatery, shop, or McDonalds to make a quick stop to get some food. Even when you're not eating your body will be grateful to for it later.

Limit your spending. This was based on the notion that if you're unable to purchase drinks, then you'll never drink alcohol! If you are planning to go to a bar take only the cash you'll need to use on drinks. It's true that this can cause some issues (especially in the event of an emergency) that's why many people bring their credit cards in case of the need to call for help'. To me, this is not a good idea: if you've had a drink or consuming alcohol, you'll want to use your card, which can be an unwise game. Today, thanks to inventions such as Apple Pay, we can make use of our smartphones to pay for purchases and we're constantly being bombarded with ways to pay for items. When it comes down to it, you must do whatever you can reduce the amount you spend: hand over your wallet to a family member to keep track of it and download an app that will limit the amount you spend on your credit card for a specific period of time and then, be sure that you will not spend more than is necessary. The key is that there is no need to spend money.

Don't be a fool! When people drink in a bar, they are likely to be more frugal. they might even offer to purchase some drinks. Under normal circumstances, you'd probably take the offer. Who would refuse anything for free? However, keep in mind we're trying to reduce our drinking and, therefore, even if we have many people around us willing to purchase drinks for us be sure to say no!

Do not get involved in rounds. Rounds are unwise because of two reasons: first they are expensive and cost lots of money and they'll result in you drinking plenty of alcohol. Imagine that you're hosting 10 guests on the night out If you're going to do rounds, that's ten drinks you'll need to purchase (think of the expense) and, on top of that, 10 drinks you've agreed to drink. If you're committed to cutting down on your drinking, stay clear of rounds as much as you can.

Know your limits. Some people are fortunate, they may get the "buzz when they drink after just one or two glasses. Some take a bit longer. You'll be able to tell what number of drinks (and what kind of drinks) it takes to feel that buzz and how long drinks you'll need until you're over the point. Keep to your limitations. Do you notice that drinking cider makes you feel uneasy in the early morning? Don't drink it. If you're feeling drunk after a glass? Do not drink a complete bottle. Every person is unique and will have their own limits however, when you're aware of yours and adhere to them, you're reducing the chance of having a hangover as well as any other health issues that may arise.

Chapter 12: The Negatives Of Alcohol/Why You Should Not Drink

There's probably over a million and one reason to decide to stop drinking, particularly if you are a regular drinker and/or are addicted to alcohol-based drinks. One of the most significant of these factors have to be related to your health. The effects of hangovers are a painful and harmful result of heavy drinking and obviously the dreaded alcohol poisoning. But they are only 2 of the many known negative effects you could endure when you consume alcohol. Alcohol addiction can impact the health of your loved ones in variety of other negative ways, too. And some of these negative consequences can be life-threatening.

Alcohol Poisoning

The effects of alcohol poisoning are more severe than any hangover and the signs can range from mild to extreme. The most severe and severe instances of alcohol poisoning could be life-threatening. The symptoms and signs of alcohol poisoning could include:

The confusion and disorientation can be a source of confusion.

Skin with a pale appearance (sometimes with a blueish tint)

Hypothermia (a reduction in the body temperature)

Stupor (unresponsiveness when conscious)

Dispensing

A strange breathing rhythm

Very slow or labored breathing

Vomiting

In some of the most severe cases of alcohol poisoning your breathing could be unable to breathe completely. It is possible to have a heart attack, get choked by your vomit, or have it be breathed into your lungs, which can cause irreparable injury. The symptoms of hypothermia may be dangerous. In addition, if you shed excess fluid and suffer from severe dehydration you could put yourself at risk of brain damage. Also, if blood glucose levels are to low levels, you may suffer from seizures.

If you have an alcohol-related poisoning that is serious enough, you may even end up in an induced coma, and then eventually die.

The effects of Alcohol on your Liver

Alcohol is harmful to many different organs of your body. One of them could be particularly harmful to is the liver. The liver is an organ of your body that frequently performs in a constant state of flux. It's the biggest organ of your body, and is responsible for around 500 distinct tasks. One of the primary tasks your liver performs is to break down food, and it converts that food into energy. In addition, your liver assists in removing your body of toxic substances. It is also an essential role in fighting off certain illnesses, specifically those that may occur within the bowel.

If your liver is damaged, you will not realize that it has been damaged until it begins to cause major issues. Drinking heavily increases the risk of developing liver disease, and can result in irreparable harm to the liver. There are a variety of causes of liver diseases, and drinking heavily can trigger what's known as "alcoholic the liver."

Oxidative stressoccurs when your liver is trying to break down its process by consuming alcohol The chemical reaction that occurs could be damaging to the cells. The damage could result in your liver become irritated and frightened to attempt to heal itself.

The toxins in the stomach bacteria, namely alcohol could cause harm to your digestive tract. The intestine lets the harmful bacteria in your gut to get into the liver. The toxins also can cause the same kind of swelling and scarring.

Consuming excessive alcohol can make your liver obese. (Quitting drinking may aid in shrinking it back in size to its original size)This is known as "fatty liver" or "steatosis." The liver converts glucose into fat, and releases it throughout the body , to keep it the time it is required.

Alcohol adversely affects the way that your liver processes fat, and causes your liver's cells to fill up with it. If this occurs to you, you could begin experiencing some kind of abdominal discomfort because your liver is swelling. It is also possible to feel sick and begin eating less. If you don't quit drinking, your liver condition will get worse and then progress to another stage of the liver condition.

You could spend 20 years destroying your liver but never feel the negative effects. The first signs of liver diseases can be:

Fatigue

Nausea

Vomiting

Diarrhea

Abdominal discomforts

In the final stages of damage to your liver, the symptoms started to become more severe, and you'll begin to notice these symptoms. These are symptoms of liver disorders referred to "alcoholic liver disease" or "fibrosis." Some signs may include:

Jaundice (yellowing of your skin)

The blood is leaking out of the bowels

Fatigue (moderate to severe)

Affluent loss and weakness

Skin itching

Easy bruising

The swelling of your ankles, legs or abdominal

Liver cancer

The gut is bleeding

A higher sensitivity to alcohol and other drugs (both recreational and medical drugs)

Your liver not being able to process any drugs

The liver is a victim of cirrhosis.

Alcohol can trigger the development of cirrhosis and quitting drinking alcohol is essential to prevent you from becoming a victim of liver failure. Liver failure occurs the time when your liver ceases completely functioning.

In the most serious cases of cirrhosis, the only method to be considered for an organ transplant is to stop abstinence from alcohol consumption for at least three months. If you stop drinking alcohol soon enough, you could reverse the liver issues due to alcohol. When you get cirrhosis your outlook will heavily depend on whether you cease drinking. If you keep drinking then you'll increase the risk of being diagnosed suffering due to liver disease.

The effects on the Brain of Alcohol On Your Brain

Alcohol consumption that is excessive can cause an imbalance of neurons off track. The neurotransmitters within your brain to transmit information at a much slower rate and make you feel very tired and sleepy. The imbalance of neurotransmitters caused by alcohol can cause changes in mood and behavior. These include:

Depression

Agitation

Memory loss

Seizures

A long-term, heavy drinking habit can result in changes to the brain's neurons, such as shrinking of brain cells. In the end, your brain's mass shrinking, and the interior area of your brain becomes bigger. This can alter a variety of your capabilities, including things such as:

Motor coordination

Control of temperature

Sleeping patterns

Mood

Cognitive functions that span a variety of areasinclude your learning abilities and memory abilities.

The neurotransmitter within your brain that are particularly vulnerable, even to alcohol in small quantities is glutamate. The glutamate is a key component of other substances in your body, however it is not as much affected by memory. Alcohol is believed to interfere with the activities of glutamates and that's likely the reason why some people are able briefly "black out" and/or forget what took place in the event that they were drinking heavily. drinking.

Alcohol also causes an increase in the serotonin release in the brain which is a different neurotransmitter which helps regulate your emotions and endorphins. Endorphins are natural compounds which can trigger feelings of happiness and euphoria after drinking alcohol. The research has revealed that the brain is trying to make up for all these changes. The neurotransmitters adjust to restore balance to your brain, despite the fact that alcohol is in the system. However, having to adapt can result in negative effects. This could result in building tolerance to alcohol, developing dependence, and feeling the symptoms of withdrawal.

The effects on Alcohol to Your Heart

Drinking alcohol can cause heart damage. The consequences of this include:

Cardiomyopathy (Stretching and/or the drooping of your heart muscle)

Arrhythmias (an irregular heartbeat)

Stroke

High blood pressure

The effects from Alcohol On Your Pancreas

Alcohol can trigger your pancreas to release toxic substances. These toxins may eventually cause a condition known as pancreatitis. Pancreatitis symptoms include the risk of a dangerous inflammation as well as an increase in the size of the veins in the pancreas that can hinder proper digestion. Damage to the pancreas can result in your body not to be able to use sugar due to its deficiency of insulin. This could lead to an illness known as "hyperglycemia." A blood sugar level that has are unbalanced could be a risky issue, especially for people with diabetes.

The effects on Alcohol On Your Bodily Systems

Central Nervous System

Alcohol is easily absorbed by your body and is able to quickly penetrate many parts within your body. These include the brain as along with other crucial areas of your body's central nervous system. It can be difficult to speak with a slurred sound in your speech, which is one of the most obvious indications that a person who has had a drink too often. It can also negative effect on your coordination and hinder your balance and your ability to walk correctly.

Alcohol consumption that is excessively high impacts how you think. Also, it affects the control of your impulses as well as your capacity to create memories. Long-term effects can result in the frontal lobes of the brain to shrink. The withdrawal symptoms of a sudden alcoholic could trigger seizures and the condition known as delirium. It may also cause permanent brain damage that, can lead to dementia.

A nerve damage can cause pain, numbness or abnormal sensations on your feet and hands. Alcoholism may cause a deficiency of the thiamine (vitamin B1). This could cause an involuntary eye movement that is rapid as well as weakness or the muscles of your eyes.

Women and men metabolize alcohol differently. It is generally less alcohol to be harmful to women.

In time, a frequent drinker can develop physically and psychologically dependent of alcohol. It could be very difficult to get control of. Contrary to the other addictions that are common the acute withdrawal from alcohol could be life-threatening. In cases of persistent, severe dependence on alcohol often require medical attention.

Digestive System

The consumption of alcohol can cause a significant negative effect on the entire of your digestive system, starting with your mouth until your colon.

Alcohol abuse can harm salivary glands as well as affect your tongue and mouth. This could lead to gum disease, tooth decay and even the loss of teeth. In addition, drinking heavily can result in the development of ulcers in your stomach, acid reflux, or heartburn. Additionally, stomach ulcers and the irritation of your stomach's liner (a condition known as gastritis) are possible.

The pancreas is a major organ that can be inflamed. It affect its capacity to assist in the digestion process and regulate the metabolism. The damage to your digestive system may result in abdominal gassiness, fullness and diarrhea. This can cause dangerous internal bleeding, which could result from hemorrhoids, ulcers, or esophageal varices triggered by cirrhosis.

Drinking alcohol can cause it to be more difficult for the stomach to absorb B Vitamins and minerals, and also to manage bacteria. People who drink a lot are more likely to have malnutrition issues, and also have an increased risk of developing cancers of the throat, mouth or esophagus, and/or colon.

Circulatory System

Alcohol can trigger the following problems with the circulatory system:

Intoxication of muscles of the heart (cardiomyopathy)

Heartbeat irregularity (arrhythmia)

High blood pressure

Stroke

Heart attack

Heart failure

People who are diabetics have an increased risk of having low blood sugar levels, especially those who are insulin users. Vitamin B6, B12 Thiamine, and Folic Acid deficiency can result in an increase in blood count. The most commonly reported signs of anemia is fatigue.

Reproductive System

One of the most frequent side effects of drinking alcohol in males is erectile dysfunction. It can cause suppression the production of hormones, alter testsicular function, and cause infertility.

Drinking excessively can cause women stop having menstrual cycles and cause women to fall pregnant. Also, it can increase the chance of having a miscarriage, premature birth or stillbirth.

Alcohol can have a very negative impact on a embryo's development. Many different developmental issues referred to as "fetal disorder of the alcohol spectrum" (FASD) (FASD) are possible. The signs of FASD may include physical impairments, emotional problems and learning issues that could persist for the entire duration of a person's life. For women, the chance to develop breast cancer is increased by drinking alcohol regularly.

Skeletal and Muscle Systems

A long-term drinking habit can make it harder for your body's ability to create and create new bone. A long-term drinking habit increases your chance of developing osteoporosis. This is the loss of bones and fractures of your bone. The muscles of your body are more susceptible to cramps, weakness and atrophy.

Immune System

If your immune system is weakened by excessive alcohol consumption and a lack of exercise, it will have a tough in fighting against viruses, germs, and nearly every type of disease. Alcoholics are more likely to contract tuberculosis or pneumonia than the other people. Drinking alcohol also increases the risk of developing types of cancer.

It sounds pretty awful, does it not? There are enough reasons to to seriously consider quitting drinking, but the fact of the matter is that it isn't ever "too too late" to stop drinking alcohol, regardless of whether you have already been diagnosed with cirrhosis of the liver or other serious medical issues.

The Detoxification Process

If an alcohol user stops drinking abruptly, they're more likely to suffer withdrawal symptoms including:

Nausea

Anxiety

Nervousness

Tremors

In some extreme instances, the symptoms may result in hallucinations, confusion (also called Delirium Tremens) as well as seizures. Detoxification from alcohol typically takes between 2 and seven days. If your withdrawal symptoms get extreme or uncomfortable There are certain drugs that your physician can prescribe to you to help you avoid them or make them much less difficult to deal with.

Chapter 13: Restitution

Humility

Be humble and ask God to take care of your weaknesses.

All of the steps require you be humble, however step 7 asks you to do this in a specific way. It is important to request your Universe and you to eliminate your flaws. Your humble heart in the sixth step has led you to the knees in step seven to ask the universe and God remove your weaknesses to enable you to make progress in your journey.

Seventh step is a symbol of total surrender. Once you have felt the freedom of confession, and the willingness to let your heart change and take the divine and universe fully into your life. It could take the person of God or take the form of accepting your new self.

Find Atonement and Meditate

In this stage you'll seek atonement for your sins via meditation. There is no need to meditate on prayer If you're uncomfortable with it however, you can simply focus on the things you'd like to manifest in your life. For instance, you could meditate with affirmations like:

I am filled with peace and joy.

I'm alcohol-free and loving life to the fullest.

I can abstain from drinking alcohol.

Through meditation, you'll be able to calm your mind and experience peace and the affirmations will strengthen your belief that you're in a position to stay away from alcohol and overcome the addiction.

Request Assistance

If you're unable to stay away from your addiction on your own Don't be afraid to contact any member of your group or your mentor and request help. You must be humble enough to admit that you're struggling in a moment, and they'll be able to assist you get through the moment. Be aware that your friends and family have been through what you're experiencing They know that you're embarrassed and embarrassed. They will be able to help you get through the situation.

Restitution

Write down all the things you've erred in and then be prepared to apologize to them for the actions you took.

Prior to your recovery your life was likely to be a storm of destructive energy that destroyed relationships and left lots of destruction left behind. Eighth step gives you the chance to go through that mess and discover something that's not broken. Rebuild anything that can be saved. Once you have felt the healing effects of the seven steps and you'll be keen to reach out to restore broken relationships with people. You will discover that making amends and not seeking advice from an advisor will be harmful to the progress you make.

You should list those who have hurt You

When you are rebuilding your relationships, you need to determine all relationships that have been damaged. It is important to note those who have hurt you and do not be caught up in feelings of anger from the people who hurt you. Before you create that list, you should first write down the people you have to be able to forgive.

Don't be shocked if names are listed on both lists. There are many who get caught in the cycle of expressing hurts and resentments with each other In order to break the cycle there must be someone willing to first forgive. Find that person.

To start the process, you'll require an eraser and an article of paper. Alongside the names of those who you need to forgiving, you must write down how you felt at the time the incidents that hurt you occurred as well as how you're still attracted to the person. This will allow you to make sure you are specific when you accept someone's forgiveness.

Write a list of those You've harmed

Make your list of people whom you have were hurt during the time. Take your time with the list and consider items that you may not have completed or neglected which could cause harm to others. Do not leave out anything that isn't important. Honesty is the best way to go for this process. Be honest about the harm that you did to those people regardless of whether it was accidentally caused by being irresponsible angry, critical and impatient or otherwise dishonorable.

Once you've compiled a list of the people you've hurt Add an additional name on your list. The name should be yours. If you indulged in your addictions, you damaged yourself as you did others who were in the same situation.

Direct Restitution

When you can, offer the necessary restitution to those who you directly harmed.

There are a few things you should be aware of as you begin the procedure of making one-on one amends with the people you've hurt. It is important to not be careless or reckless when trying to get your revenge. It's crucial to avoid putting off this step. Many recovering addicts will fall back due to the fears of finishing step nine. Talk to an advisor if that you need assistance with this particular step.

You may find yourself attracted to not meet with people who is on the list. Beware of this except for a legal requirement that prevents you from them. A spirit of honesty and humility can repair broken relationships if you take the time to meet the person in person. Make them aware that you're contacting them to seek amends. Be respectful of their decision not to visit you if they do wish to discuss the issue. If they offer you the opportunity, be specific and concise in your apology. The details are not needed for this situation.

The goal is not to discuss your view of the issue. It's about admitting that you made a mistake and apologize and then make any restitution you are able to. Don't argue with someone , or criticize them when they don't have an open or friendly answer. Befriend them with a attitude with humility, and propose forgiveness and not justifying.

Resolving to apologize for certain mistakes can be a challenge. For instance, if you are required to apologize for something that could result in legal implications, such as an egregious sexual offense or dishonesty, you could be tempted give an excuse or to avoid making amends. It is recommended to seek out professional advice prior to taking actions in cases of serious nature such as this.

Sometimes there may not be an option of making amends in person. It could be that the person is deceased or you may not know the location where they reside. In such cases you may still be able to pay the restitution informally. You can send an email to express your sorrow and desire of being remorseful, even when your letter isn't able to be handed over. You could also give a donation to the charity that this person is a fan of. Find people who remind you of their name and aid the person. You can also offer help to an individual in your family in a private way.

There are instances when asking someone else to make changes could hurt the person, or be harmful to the person. If you believe this is the case, talk about it with an advisor and find out what they believe you should do. This phase of process should not lead to the harm of another person. There are instances where you may have caused harm beyond the repair capabilities of your body.

If you are able to make amends for past mistakes there are some people that you're unable to deal with. Don't despair. Numerous people have faced the same issue as you do. Talk about your feelings with your counselor and be sincere. If you're still feeling scared or anger towards the person, then you ought to put off your appointment with them. Look for positive reasons for why reconciling and making amends could aid. If you are able to do these things and remain open to change, you might be in a position to be able to reconcile with the person in the future.

Be Kind to Others and Avoid Judgment

This is when you cease judging others for their actions and focus on the actions you take. Recognize that they require compassion and understanding just as you did when you recovered. It is a great time to get out and help out at homeless shelters as well as animal shelters in order to give back to the community you live in. Get involved in the community once again, so that you feel valued and feel like you're acting in the best way.

When someone approaches you with a question Be the person who listens and provides them with gentle advice about how to approach an issue. You're now the person who is sponsoring them at this moment.

Chapter 14: Understanding Alcohol

Alcohol is a legally-produced substance that eases stress and inhibits. It has a variety of effects that range including poor coordination and conversations that are slurred. It is not the case that everyone who drinks is an alcoholic, however any person whose life is negatively impaired by the consumption of alcohol can be categorized as having a problem with alcohol. Alcohol consumption is typically in the form of a glass or two in various forms, which includes wine, ale and hard liquor.

Abuse and craving for beer

Beer is an alcoholic beverage composed of water that is normal barley, hops, and yeast. When compared to wines and hard liquor beers have the lowest alcohol content per unit (ABV). Beer's ABV can vary from two to twelve percent and the most commonly consumed beer (Budweiser, Coors Light, Miller Lite,

Corona, Busch and so on.) being in the range of 4 to 6 percent alcohol.

Drinking games with beer have become commonplace in the universities of the U.S and the growth of craft beer has brought beer drinking into fashion with microbreweries and home brewers pushing the boundaries of new flavors and taste that are being introduced. Another side effect from the revolution in ale is that some beers might contain higher levels of alcohol when compared to usual home brew Some are as high as 11% or even 12 percent.

The same goes for those who drink at events with friends or who only drink craft beers are more susceptible to an alcohol dependence disorder. In the meantime, it's the case there are "cultural drinkers" remain in the habit of drinking even when everyone else has quit drinking.

Abuse of alcohol and dependence on wine

Wine is made from fermented grapes, or other fruits like fruit berries or pomegranates; typically it is sold either red or white, with various flavors. Chardonnay, Pinot Grigio, Riesling and Moscato are white wines, while Merlot, Cabernet, Pinot noir and Zinfandel are reds.

Different types of wine made from grapes

In comparison to beer, wine contain a higher amount of alcohol. The average dose of wine (5oz) is based on the drinking alcohol content in 12 ounces of alcohol. Wines are usually consumed at dinner parties or served with crackers and cheese; its reputation being an "elegant" drink is difficult to discern when someone is addicted to it.

Women comprise 59% of wine consumption in U.S and are the primary intended audience for ads advertising the beverage. Women are less musculoskeletal and have less water within their bodies. When drinking wine, the alcohol dilutes the alcohol, meaning women have higher levels of alcohol bloodstreams as compared to males. This causes women to become more impaired , and also exposes their brains as well as other organs to more alcohol-related damage when they consume wine. This is why women are more susceptible to developing alcohol dependence, however, both genders can experience problems with wine.

You or someone else you care about is a wine addict and regularly drinks it, or is using it to avoid depression or stress, then it is possible that addiction is lurking and you must seek immediate assistance for any wine dependence.

Alcohol consumption and abuse

Liquor is the generic term for spirits or hard drinks such as vodka, tequila spirits like gin, rum and whiskey. Alcohol is a stronger ABV than wine or ale and is typically mixed with sodas, juices or water. The standard dose of liquor is 1.5 to 2 ounces. Carbonation increases the absorption rate of alcohol into the bloodstream. Therefore, mixing soda with alcohol can cause a faster intoxication. The less alcohol amount makes them more enjoyable to drink, resulting in more risk of abuse and drunkenness. A lot of long-time drinkers identify different types of alcohol with different sensations of intoxication. However, technology is yet to establish this, and studies have shown that alcohol has the same effects on all regardless of the type of drink consumed.

The setting in which the alcohol is consumed could influence the perception of being intoxicated. Someone drinking an alcoholic drink at dinner will more likely to feel a sense of happiness and exhaustion when drinking tequila in an event with a lot of energy can cause an entirely different type of alcohol-induced euphoria.

Individuals with a severe alcohol disorder might believe that they are unable to begin their day without a sip of vodka, or that they are unable to complete the day without a glass of whiskey. No matter what kind of liquor consumed, any type of alcohol is capable of becoming addictive.

Understanding Binge Drinking

The binge drinking subset is people who drink five or more gallons of alcohol, or women who drink four drinks or more in the span of two hours.

A frequent drinker of alcohol will likely stop his or her alcohol consumption; a person who's addicted may want to consume all their drinks and might require assistance to quit A prolonged bout of drinking could lead to alcoholism.

The immediate after-effects of Alcohol

Alcoholic drinks are an important central nervous system (CNS) depressant, meaning that it reduces physical and mental movements. drinkers might experience a reduction in feelings of anxiety or anxiety. It is generally referred to as an energizer, which means that drinkers feel more confident at an event and less worried about what others think of their drinking.

Since drinking alcohol is generally legal and accepted across many societies, it can be difficult to discern the difference between its legal usage and abuse. In general, any use of alcohol that results in negative consequences is regarded as the use of alcohol for abuse. Some of the negative consequences of alcohol are:

physical injury or an illness.

Reliable relationships.

Workplace problems.

Financial difficulty.

If the abuse is increasingly frequent, the situation can turn into addiction.

Dependence on Alcohol

Alcoholic addiction, also referred to as alcoholism, is the result of the desire to drink alcohol drinks, as well as having the ability to avoid drinking, even when it can cause severe harm to oneself or others. Signs of alcoholism can include eating more food than is necessary and a desire to stay away from drinking, but struggling with becoming tolerant to alcohol consumption, experiencing a relapse in which personal and professional obligations to be ruined by the effects of alcohol and drinking alcohol.

High-Functioning Alcoholics

There's a distinct category of alcoholics known by the term "high-functioning" alcoholics. People who are high-functioning alcohol addicts stop their addiction from impacting their lives at work and in their private lives.

A New York article estimated that up to 50% of all alcohol users are high-functioning alcohol users. Professors, lawyers and doctors comprise an important portion of people. Alcoholics who are high-functioning do not realize that they are suffering until they confront serious effects of drinking. The danger of having a high-functioning addiction is that it can persist for a long period of period of time without realizing that they have issues.

Alcoholic drinks and other substances

As it is the norm in our society alcohol drinks are more likely to be used in conjunction with other drugs. Like the CNS stimulant, alcohol can pose an increased risk when mixed with other substances including benzodiazepines as well as various painkillers. Consuming alcohol on its own is risky, but mixing it with other chemicals could be deadly.

What is an Alcohol Use Disorder?

A lot of Americans in U.S finish their day by drinking a glass of beer or wine. But how do they tell when they've surpassed their alcoholic limit? What can you do to tell if you've reached the limit of alcohol consumption (AUD) threshold? (AUD)?

Drinking "in moderate quantities" means that you should have only one drink a day if female and two drinks if you're male. One drink equals:

1.5 1 ounces of alcohol (like whisky, rum or even tequila).

5 Ounces of wine.

12-ounces beer.

Another way to look at how you consume alcohol is to look at the typical amount of alcohol you drink in a given week.

Women "heavy" (or "hazardous" drinking refers to a lot of more than 7 drinks a week, or more than three in a single day. For males, it's over 14 drinks per week and more than four per day.

Alcoholic Use Disorder

Dangerous drinking may be the result of a condition known as alcohol dependence disorder. It's a chronic illness that impacts the brain. Around 16 million people - both children and adults within the U.S. have it. If your parents' genes could put you at risk as well as your psychological and physical surroundings can make you vulnerable.

There are many signs that could indicate an individual is affected by AUD. Some of the signs include:

An uncontrollable urge to drink.

Inability to control the amount you consume.

Negative thoughts that you don't drink.

Drinking alcohol in dangerous situations.

Drinking alcohol that doesn't lead to accountability.

It is a sin to drink even though it can cause problems or make the problem more severe.

Inattention to activities that are important because of drinking alcohol.

There are mild or moderate forms of AUD. It all is based on the symptoms you're experiencing. It is more likely that you have AUD when any of the following occur.

It's impossible to rest or relax without drinking.

It is essential to drink a glass of water to get you started on your day.

Drinking is the only way in order to make yourself social.

Alcohol can be a method to forget your troubles.

You drive after drinking.

It is common to mix alcohol with other substances.

You shouldn't drink when you're nursing or pregnant. baby.

If your family members ask you about how much you drink, you're not going to lie about it.

People are hurt or angry after drinking.

It's difficult to recall what you were drinking when you're drunk.

Your responsibility is weakened due to the alcohol you consume.

Drinking and drinking has caused legal issues.

You've tried to stay away from drinking, but you've did not succeed.

It's not a good idea to stop drinking.

To feel the effects of alcohol, you need to drink more and more.

You may experience symptoms such as nausea, shakiness and shakiness problems, seizures and more when you stop drinking for a few days. The more symptoms you experience in your body, the more serious your AUD may be.

The effects of the AUD

Even if the condition you are experiencing is not severe, it can be a major influence on your mental and physical well-being.

For certain, AUD could cause:

Memory loss.

Hangovers.

Blackouts.

The long-term results are:

Stomach problems.

Heart issues.

Cancer.

Brain damage.

Memory loss over the long term.

Pancreatitis.

Blood pressure that is high.

Cirrhosis or damage to the liver

There's a chance that you'll be in danger, which can increase your risk of being injured or dying:

Car accidents.

Homicide.

Suicide.

Then I fell asleep.

The effects of AUD can affect your family members too and your drinking could affect your relationships with your family members due to anger issues or neglect, and abuse. Women who are pregnant are at risk of the possibility of having a miscarriage. Their child is more likely to be diagnosed with the fatal condition known as alcohol-related syndrome, and an increased chance of suffering from SIDS.

Chapter 15: Dealing With Peer Pressure

Peer pressure, despite being thought of as something that is only affecting preteens to young adults is actually quite common and subtle. It is all about the words spoken to a certain type of person and at what time.

What I am referring to is: If an older high school student were to chat with an freshman girl, her peers were not around her (they continued to move when she stopped) and then said, "Hey, do you like to have a beverage?" ... What would you say that happened the next day?

Some people are not able to resist this kind of pressure. Some people are extremely determined and will do whatever they can to uphold their convictions. However, once they're in a new place and feels that the ground around them might shake or push them to the ground at any time and they're more likely to take every step to get to the ground they're on and be amid the other people.

However, the majority of people, particularly those who are young, are becoming more anxious as they learn more regarding what they will be doing in their "future duties" ("To be an excellent wife and please the spouse." "Man take a step up Stop looking vulnerable." "You'll have to be the one to do this in the future." ."). This puts an enormous amount of pressure for a young person with an inherently transforming mind to conform to the mold of society or be a snob and never have anyone take care of you.

Yes, it's like a dramatic situation, but it's actually the way people feel in these roles. Humans want affection and be part of a community. It is possible to die due to the lack of contact when we are infants and our health may actually decrease if we don't get any kind of contact in a single day, which is why it's vital for many reasons. It's an instinct of survival encoded in our genes to find people and connect with them. Even in our adulthood we are still able to experience the same kinds of thoughts in our minds due to the way we're programmed to operate.

How is one supposed to respond to the pressures of peer pressure, especially those who tend to respond "Yes" to any request they are asked or aren't comfortable in social settings?

Attend an event with people you are confident in

You can trust lots of individuals, but the type of people I'm speaking of are those you are able to keep close when you attend a party or social event , and will not be pressured to do something. An easy "yes" and "no" inquiry could be requested, but they'll honor your decision. They'll also not leave you alone (if you're part of an ensemble; however, when you're in a couple it's more likely to happen if both of you are looking to pursue separate interests).

Keep your eyes open for people who are similar to you.

I'm not talking about people who behave or speak in the same manner. I'm talking about those with similar goals to you. In this situation, it could be to stay with designated drivers or those who don't drink at a particular time. They'll not only be there to keep you in the company of others, but also have a reason to stop drinking, a less urge for drinking, as well as a group of people to share your laughter over the drunken actions with. There are certain people can be crazy after drinking. There's always some interesting things happening in an event with enough alcohol to get people drunk.

Increase your self-confidence and self-esteem.

This can take longer and more effort achieve in case you're not doing enough of it. Being confident in your decisions and choices can aid you in being in a position to defend yourself when someone wants for something you're not willing to do. If someone asks you to drink or insists on drinking and be confident, being confident can allow you say "No thank you I'm not interested in one" and leave when needed.

Refraining from the group in this situation will require a significant amount of courage, yet it's probably also among the most beneficial actions to take when dealing to peer pressure. The process of getting out of the way you are feeling pressured, regardless of whatever you're being forced to do in this particular social setting must always be the first priority over the feelings of the other person.

One exception is that you may enjoy it, and this could turn risky quickly. If that's the case you must draw the attention of people around your by speaking louder and making eye contact with people, or repeating the same phrase repeatedly ("No I'm not going to be doing that, not ask me") or should, if necessary, make the scene. It's not in the same way as alcohol does however there is an expectation on females, especially drinking to the point that they can make a profit of your vulnerability. There are many benefits when you are in the same group and having confidence there.

The process of building them will aid you in many other aspects of your identity as well as your daily life! With more confidence, you'll be more at ease with yourself and let you feel as if you're more able to travel across the globe. It gives you the confidence to seek to speak with someone, ask for a position you're not certain of landing and also to ask for an increase in your salary or promotion in certain situations!

Being able to stand with your own beliefs because you're confident in how you conduct yourself in the world is crucial to be a part of this particular culture, or to tear someone down in order to build yourself. Help others by lifting them up to ensure that everyone is more comfortable and confident than before.

Beware of the lies

This is especially true for people who are younger however, if someone ever claims, "Everyone does this thing nowadays!" ... It's definitely exaggerating. There are far too many people to do the exact thing. This kind of comment could make one feel that it's better to stick along with what is being imposed by the system because of this.

Be sure to stand up for yourself. Do not feel inferior since "every" person among your friends does something. It's true that many people are making up stories to appear more mature or younger when they're in one scenarios like these. Yes, it's possible that everybody at a party drinks a little alcohol. But that doesn't mean they're completely drunk or drinking something difficult, like vodka. It's normal to mix drinks in a small amount or take a small amount of alcohol, followed by other drinks, such as soda or water.

Another method of determining the truth in this particular scenariois to determine how drunk someone else is. If someone demands you drink however, you can't find the cup they have for themselves this is a red signal to not take the cup. If they're drunk and insisting that you drink the reason is likely that they are also looking for an additional drink and think that everyone should have drinks.

Chapter 16: Alcohol Withdrawal Syndrome

Alcohol withdrawal syndrome is a risk of becoming fatal. It is a possibility for those who have been drinking a lot of alcohol for a long time, perhaps months or even a single week. They after which they either stop drinking completely or drastically reduce their alcohol consumption.

It is possible to experience withdrawal symptoms due to alcohol as little as two hours after the last drink. The symptoms can range from mild anxiety and shakiness to more severe issues such as DT (delirium of tremens) and seizures may last for a number of weeks. There is an estimated one to five percent mortality rate due to DT that is typically manifested by high fever, rapid heartbeat, and confusion. It is crucial to get medical attention if you begin to notice symptoms of alcohol withdrawal because the symptoms that appear to be to be mild may quickly get worse. There is a way to reduce the risk for developing DT and withdrawal-related seizures by undergoing treatments for withdrawal from alcohol that are suitable for you. Also, I want to stress the importance of seeking out your doctor if you've had prior alcohol withdrawal symptoms or suffer from any other health issues, such as seizures or lung diseases and heart disease as well as infections. Be aware that serious withdrawal symptoms from alcohol are a medical emergencies. If you or someone else in your family suffer from seizures, irregular heartbeats, hallucinations, extreme confusion or fever, call 911 immediately or visit the emergency department.

What are the causes of withdrawal from alcohol?

The brain chemicals that send messages, also known as neurotransmitters, are affected when you drink an extended period of excessive drinking. This is particularly the case in the case of excessive drinking each day. Alcohol can enhance your effects from GABA which is a neurotransmitter that produces feelings of relaxation and calm. However, prolonged drinking will eventually reduce GABA activities , which leads you to need ever more alcohol to get the results you seek.

The habitual drinking of alcohol also reduces the functioning that this neurotransmitter (known in the term glutamate) that triggers emotions of excitability. To ensure equilibrium the glutamate system responds by operating at a higher rate than it typically does to help moderate drinking and nondrinkers.

If a person who is drinking heavily cuts down or abruptly ceases their alcohol consumption and the neurotransmitters previously suppressed by alcohol have been released. What happens is that neurotransmitters produce an increase in their levels, which causes the phenomenon known as brain hyperexcitability. The symptoms associated with withdrawal like DT seizures, tremor, seizure anxiety, agitation, and anxiety are not in line with the effects of drinking alcohol.

The intensity of the signs of withdrawal dependent on the length of time and how much you've consumed. A few minor symptoms may occur within 6 to 12 hours following the stoppage of drinking. There are instances when individuals may be able to determine their blood alcohol level when one of the following symptoms start with shaky hands, insomnia and sweating, headaches nausea, vomiting and moderate anxiety.

In the 12 hours following one day following the last drink they had, alcoholics might experience visually, auditory or tactile hallucinations that typically last within two days. This isn't really as common to hallucinations that are associated to DT even though it's called alcoholic hallucinosis. Many people are aware of the perception that these bizarre experiences aren't true.

Between one and two days after an alcohol user stops drinking, withdrawal symptoms usually begin to occur. However, they can occur at any time, as early as 2 days after drinking the last one. Individuals who have had multiple detoxifications previously have more risk of developing seizures.

DT usually begins within 2 to 3 days following having had your last drink. It is possible to have higher risk of DT in the event that you suffer from one or more of the risk factors listed below such as a experience with DT or withdrawal seizures abnormal liver function, acute medical conditions. The symptoms of DT generally peak around the fifth day of the week: Low grade fever, severe anxiety as well as confusion, disorientation and hallucinations that aren't able to be identified from reality, an irregular heartbeat and a racing beat excessive sweating, seizures and high blood pressure.

What is the alcohol withdrawal Syndrome characterized?

In the event that your medical professional suspects you suffer with alcohol withdrawal, he will request your entire medical history, including the quantity of alcohol consumed and how long has gone by since you last stopped drinking, and the length of time you've been drinking. It will also ask whether you've ever had any previous experiences with withdrawal from alcohol or if you suffer from any medical or psychiatric conditions, and whether you're abusing other substances.

Following the appointment your doctor will then proceed with a physical exam in order to determine any withdrawal symptoms that you may be experiencing as well as any medical issues that could cause symptoms, such as pancreatitis, irregular heartbeats, nerve system impairment, congestive cardiac insufficiency, liver disease, inflammation of the coronary vessels,, and gastrointestinal bleeding. Your doctor might also prescribe blood tests to assess your liver function , and also measure your electrolyte and alcohol levels as well as your complete blood count. It is also possible to undergo an urine test to determine whether you are taking prescription drugs or other illicit substances.

A doctor makes his or her determination as to whether you suffer from an alcohol-related withdrawal disorder and the severity it is, based on the outcomes of your medical history, physical exam , and laboratory tests.

What is the best way to treat Alcohol Withdrawal Syndrome treated?

Most often the doctor will offer you an outpatient treatment when you experience mild or moderate withdrawal symptoms. This is especially true when your doctor is aware that you have a large family and friends to help you through treatment. The outpatient approach is preferred by many patients due to it being not just viewed as less costly when compared to detoxification inpatients, but also safe and effective.

The doctor could ask you to receive inpatient treatment when he or she believes that you don't have a an adequate and reliable system which can assist you during treatment. Inpatient therapy is also recommended for pregnant women and women who have suffered from any of these previously: specific medical or psychiatric diseases and severe withdrawal symptoms. numerous detoxifications previously experienced as well as DT or withdrawal seizures.

There are three main goals for treatment of withdrawal: lessen acute withdrawal symptoms, stop more complications and commence long-term treatment for encouraging abstinence from alcohol.

Conclusion

I hope I could help you to understand what alcohol dependence is and what do next to get rid of it completely. The issue is that, when you don't admit that you're suffering from a problem and admit it, your family members will suffer. Are you aiming to let go of your loved ones? Perhaps you aren't aware of it, but the alcohol is slowly separating people you love , but who struggle with the self-destructive path you've chosen to follow to live your daily life. It is imperative to act nowor else you could lose them.

The next step is applying the advice I've provided in this book to ensure that you can lead the most satisfying and happy life.

The problem is that those who drink heavily on a regular regularly are usually living in a reality that isn't entirely real. They aren't able to blame themselves for things that happen to be wrong. They search for reasons. It's time to own up and admit that there is an issue as, until you do not even begin to figure out the solution.

www.ingramcontent.com/pod-product-compliance
Lightning Source LLC
Chambersburg PA
CBHW071835080526
44589CB00012B/1007